Hugh Hamilton, John Adams, Charles F. Adams

Philosophical Essays

on the Following Subjects - I. On the principles of mechanics. II On the

ascent of vapours, the formation of clouds, rain and dew, and on several

other phaenomena of air and water. III. Observations and conjectures on

the nature

Hugh Hamilton, John Adams, Charles F. Adams

Philosophical Essays
on the Following Subjects - I. On the principles of mechanics. II On the ascent of
vapours, the formation of clouds, rain and dew, and on several other phaenomena
of air and water. III. Observations and conjectures on the nature

ISBN/EAN: 9783337348069

Printed in Europe, USA, Canada, Australia, Japan

Cover: Foto ©Thomas Meinert / pixelio.de

More available books at **www.hansebooks.com**

PHILOSOPHICAL
E S S A Y S

On the following Subjects:

I.
On the Principles of MECHANICS.

II.
On the Afcent of VAPOURS, the Formation of CLOUDS, RAIN and DEW, and on feveral other Phænomena of AIR and WATER.

III.
Obfervations and Conjectures on the Nature of the AURORA BOREALIS, and the Tails of COMETS.

BY

HUGH HAMILTON, D.D. F.R.S.
Profeffor of Philofophy in the Univerfity of Dublin.

DUBLIN:

Printed by W. SLEATER, at POPE's HEAD, on CORK-HILL. 1766.

TO

The Right Honourable

FRANCIS ANDREWS, L.L.D.

PROVOST of TRINITY COLLEGE, DUBLIN,

AND

One of his Majefty's Moft Honourable PRIVY COUNCIL,

The following

E S S A Y S

Are humbly Infcribed,

By his moft faithful

And obedient Servant,

The AUTHOR.

AN

ESSAY

ON THE

PRINCIPLES of MECHANICS.

A N

E S S A Y

O N

The Principles of Mechanics.*

N this Eſſay I mean only to offer ſome Remarks on the Methods that have been commonly uſed in treating of thoſe Engines that are called the Mechanic Powers; and to give an Account of the Principles on which, I think, we may beſt explain their Nature and Manner of Acting.

* This Eſſay was read at a Meeting of the Royal Society on the 21ſt and 28th of *April*, 1763, communicated in a Letter dated 13 *July*, 1762, to *Matthew Raper*, Eſq; F. R. S. of *Thorley*, in *Hertfordſhire*. *Vide* Phil. Tranſactions. Vol. LIII.

The

The many ufeful Inftruments that have been fo ingenioufly invented, and fo fuccefsfully executed, and the great Perfection to which the Mechanic Arts are now arrived, would naturally incline one to think that the true Principles on which the Efficacy and Operations of the feveral Machines depend, muft long fince have been accurately explained. But this is by no Means a neceffary Inference; for, however Men may differ in their Opinions about the true Method of accounting for the Effects of the feveral Machines, yet the practical Principles of Mechanics are fo perfectly known by Experience and Obfervation, that the Artift is thereby enabled to contrive and adjuft the movements of his Engines with as much certainty and fuccefs as he could do, were he thoroughly acquainted with the Laws of Motion, from which thefe Principles may be ultimately derived. However, tho' an enquiry into the true Method of deducing the practical Principles of Mechanics from the Laws of Motion, fhould perhaps not contribute much to promote the Progrefs of the Mechanic Arts, yet it is an Enquiry in itfelf ufeful, and in fome Meafure neceffary; for, fince late Authors have ufed very different Methods of treating this Subject, it may be fuppofed that no one Method has been looked upon as fatisfactory and unexceptionable. I fhould therefore wifh to contribute towards having this Subject treated with more accuracy than has been hitherto done.

The

The moſt general and remarkable theorem in Mechanics certainly is this, " That when two " Weights, by means of a Machine counterpoiſe " each other, and are then made to move toge- " ther, their Quantities of Motion will be equal". Now an *Æquilibrium* always accompanying this equality ot Motions, bears ſuch a reſemblance to the Caſe wherein two moving Bodies ſtop each other, when they meet together with equal Quantities of Motion; that Doƈtor *Wallis*, and after him moſt of the late Writers, have thought the Cauſe of an *Æquilibrium* in the ſeveral Machines, might be immediately aſſigned; by ſaying, That ſince one Body cannot produce in another a Quantity of Motion equal to its own, without loſing its own at the ſame Time; two heavy Bodies, counteraƈting each other by means of a Machine muſt continue at reſt, when they are ſo circumſtanced that one cannot deſcend, without cauſing the other to aſcend, at the ſame Time, and with the ſame Quantity ot Motion, and therefore two heavy Bodies in ſuch Caſes muſt always counterbalance each other. Now this Argument would be a juſt one, if it could properly be ſaid that the Motion of the aſcending Body was produced by that of the deſcending one; but, ſince the Bodies are ſo conneƈted that one cannot poſſibly begin to move before the other, I apprehend, that, if the Bodies are ſuppoſed to move, it cannot be ſaid that the Motion of one is produced by that of the other:

B 2 ſince

since whatever Force is suppofed to move one muft be the immediate Caufe of Motion in the other alfo; that is, both their Motions muft be fimultaneous Effects of the fame Caufe, juft as if the two Bodies were really but one. And therefore if I was to fuppofe, in this Cafe, that the fuperior Weight of the heavier Body (which may be in itfelf much more than able to fuftain the lighter) fhould overcome the Weight of the lighter and produce equal Motions in both Bodies; I do not think that from thence I could be reduced to the Abfurdity of fuppofing, that one Body, by its Motion, might produce in another a Motion equal to its own, and yet not lofe its own at the fame time. But thofe who argue from the equality of Motions on this Occafion fay further, that, fince the two Bodies muft have equal Motions when they do move, they muft have equal Endeavours to move even whilft they are at reft, and therefore thefe Endeavours to move, being equal and contrary, muft deftroy each other, and the Bodies muft continue at reft, and confequently balance each other. In Anfwer to this I muft obferve, that the abfolute Force with which a heavy Body endeavours to defcend from a State of reft can only be proportionable to its Weight; and therefore I think it is neceffary that fome Caufe fhould be affigned why (for Inftance in the Lever) the endeavour of one Pound to defcend fhall be equal to that of four Pounds; and efpecially as the *Fulcrum* on which both weights

act

act requires no greater Force to support it than that of five Pounds.

From thefe Confiderations I infer, that the Reafon why very unequal Weights may balance each other, fhould be affigned not from their having equal *momenta* when made to move together, but by proving *a priori* without confidering their Motions, that either the Reaction of the fixed Parts of the Machine, or fome other Caufe, fo far takes off from the Weight of the heavier Body as to leave it only juft able to fupport the lighter. However, as this Equality of *momenta* which always accompanies an *Æquilibrium*, affords a very elegant Theorem, it ought to be taken Notice of in every Treatife of Mechanics, and may ferve as an *Index* of an *Æquilibrium*. But I would not have it applied to a Purpofe for which it is unfit; as it has been in another Inftance by Doctor *Keil*, who from thence gives the Reafon why Water ftands at the fame height in a narrow Tube and a wide Veffel with which it communicates. And an Argument of the fame kind is applied ftill more improperly by Dr. *Rutherforth* and others, to fhew why a drop of Water included in a fmall conical Tube will move towards the narrower End; and yet the true Ways of accounting for both thefe Phæno-mena are extremely obvious and eafy.

The

The fimple Mechanic Powers are ufually reck-oned fix, the Lever, Axle and Wheel, Pully, Wedge, inclined Plane, and Screw. The only Method I have met with of explaining the Nature of thefe Machines upon one and the fame Principle, is that which I juft now examined ; and, as that appears to me unfatisfactory, I fhall confider the Nature of each Machine feparately in the Order I have fet them down.

The Lever is faid to be a right Line, inflexible and void of weight. Its fundamental Property is this ; when any two Forces act' againft each other on the Arms of a Lever, they will continue in *Æquilibrio*, if their Quantities are inverfely as the Diftances between the Points to which they are ap-plied and the Point round which the Lever turns, which Point is called the *Fulcrum* or Prop.

Several Methods have been ufed, by different Authors, to prove, that this Property muft necefla-rily belong to the Lever. We find, in the Works of *Archimedes*, a Proof brought for this Purpofe, which has fince been made ufe of by feveral Writers of Mechanics; who, I find, have fome-what altered the Form of his Argument, the Sub-ftance of which is generally expreffed as follows, —" When a Cylinder of any uniform Matter is " fupported at its middle Point, it will continue

" at

" at reſt; for all the Parts on one Side muſt ba-
" lance thoſe on the other, being exactly equal
" to them both in weight and ſituation, ſo that the
" whole weight of this Cylinder may be looked upon
" as acting on the middle Point on which it is ſup-
" ported. From whence it follows, that the
" Weight of ſuch a Cylinder will act upon what-
" ever ſupports it, in the ſame Manner as it would
" do if it was all contracted into the middle Point
" of its Axis. If therefore we ſuppoſe the Cy-
" linder to be diſtinguiſhed into two unequal Cy-
" linders or Segments, the Diſtances between the
" midde Points of thoſe Segments and the Middle
" of the whole Cylinder will be inverſely as the
" lengths of the Segments; that is, inverſely as
" their Weights: But, as it was ſaid above, the
" weight of each Cylinder acts in the ſame Man-
" ner as it would do if contracted into the middle
" Point of its Axis; and therefore if the Weights
" of thoſe Cylinders be contracted into theſe
" Points, they will continue to ſupport each, as
" before. And thence it is concluded, that any
" two Weights acting againſt each other on a Line
" ſuſtained at a fixed point, will counterpoiſe one
" another, when they are inverſely as the Dif-
" tances of the Points on which they act, from
" the Point on which the Line reſts." To this
Agreement there ſeems to be a manifeſt Objection;
for, when the whole Cylinder is diſtinguiſhed into
two Segments, part of the Weight of the greater
Segment

Segment acts on the fame Side of the *Fulcrum*
with the leffer Segment ; and therefore when the
whole Weight of the greater Segment is contracted into its middle Point on one Side of the Ful-
cram, and acts all of it againft the leffer Segment,
it requires at leaft fome Proof to fhew, that this
contracted Weight will be balanced by the
Weight of the leffer Segment. Mr. *Hugens*, in
his *Mifcellaneous Obfervations on Mechanics*, takes
Notice of this Objection to *Archimedes*'s Method,
which, he fays, feveral Mathematicians had endeavoured to remove, but without Succefs. He therefore, inftead of this Method, propofed one of his
own, which depends on a *Poftulatum* that he ufes in
common with *Archimedes*, and which I think ought
not to be granted on this Occafion; it is this :
" When equal Bodies are placed on the Arms of a
" Lever, the one which is furtheft from the *Fulcrum*
" will prevail and raife the other up." Now this
is taking it for granted, in other Words, that a
fmall Weight placed further from the *Fulcrum*
will fupport or raife a greater one. The Caufe and
Reafon of which Fact muft be derived from the
Demonftration that follows, and therefore this Demonftration ought not to be founded on the fup·
pofed felf-evidence of what is partly the Thing to
be proved: But perhaps it may be faid, that the
Poftulatum may be granted merely on this Account ;
That the Center of Gravity of the two Bodies
(which in this Cafe is the middle Point between
them)

them) is not fuftained; and therefore the Body which is on the fame Side of the *Fulcrum* with the Center of Gravity will defcend.

In Anfwer to which I muft obferve, that this Property, which the Center of Gravity has of defcending, when not placed directly above or below the Point of Sufpenfion, cannot be proved to belong to it in any Cafe, nor can we even fhew that there is only one Center of Gravity between two Bodies joined by a right Line, until it is proved in general that the Center of Gravity of any two Bodies is a Point fo placed between them that their Diftances from it are inverfely as their Weights: but this in effect includes the principal Property of the Lever, which therefore cannot be proved from any previous Suppofition, that the Center of Gravity will defcend, even when the Bodies are equal, and we know it is the middle Point between them.

I muft now proceed to confider what Sir *Ifaac Newton* hath delivered on this Subject in his *Principia*, after the 2d cor. to the 3d Law of Motion which Dr. *Clarke* (in his Notes on *Rohault*) and all the fubfequent Writers, have quoted as an elegant Proof of the Property of the Lever; and therefore what appears to me at prefent an Objection to this Proof I fhall mention with great diffidence, and in hopes of being fet right if I am wrong. Sir *Ifaac*

C   fuppofes

ſuppoſes two Weights, as A and P. Fig. 1. to hang
by Threads, from the Points M and N. in a
Wheel or circular Plane Perpendicular to the Horizon and Movable about its Center O; and then
propoſes to determine the Forces with which theſe
Weights act to turn the Wheel round its Center.
In order to do this, he ſuppoſes that it is indiffer-
ent from what Points in the perpendicular Lines
M A and N P the Weights are hung, for that they
will ſtill have the ſame Power to turn the Wheel
about its Center. His Words are : " *Quoniam nil*
" *refert utrum filorum puncta K, L, D, affixa ſint*
" *vel non affixa ad planum rotæ ; pondera idem valebunt*
" *ac ſi ſuſpenderentur a punctis K et L, vel D et L.*"
Now whether the Points of the Threads K, L, D,
are fixed or not to the Plane of the Wheel is certainly of Importance, as it muſt make a Difference in the Points of Suſpenſion of the Weights,
and conſequently in the Degrees of Obliquity
with which the Weights act ; for the loweſt Point
of the Thread that is fixed to the Plane muſt be
conſidered as the Point from which the Weight
hangs ; as the Parts of the Thread above that
Point are quite uſeleſs not being at all acted upon.
And from thence I ſhall endeavor to ſhew that to
ſuppoſe the Weight A will have the ſame Power
to turn the Wheel from whatever Point in the Line
M A it hangs, is in Effect preſuppoſing what is
intended to be proved. For it appears, from what
he ſays immediately after, that, when the Weight

A

A hangs from the Point D, if its whole Force be exprefled by the Line A D, and be refolved into two Forces, D C and A C, the former only will have any Effect in turning the Wheel, as it acts perpendicularly on the *Radius* O D, while the latter is loft, its Direction being parallel to O D. But it is evident, that, when the fame Weight hangs from the Point K, as it acts perpendicularly on the *Radius* O K, its whole Force is exerted to turn the Wheel, and none of it loft by oblique Action. Therefore the Force which the Weight A, exerts to oppofe the Weight P, and turn the Wheel when it hangs from D, is, to the Force it exerts when it hangs from K, as the Line D C to A D, or as O K, to O D, (fim. Triang. A D C, D O K) that is the Force exerted by the Weight A, hanging from the Points D and K, are inverfely as the *Radii* O D, and O K. And therefore to fuppofe, that thefe two Forces will have the fame Effect in turning the Wheel and oppofing the Weight P, is the fame as fuppofing that two Forces will have equal Effects in moving the Arms of a Lever (on which they act perpendicularly) when they are inverfely as the Lengths of thofe Arms.——But this is the very Conclufion Sir *Ifaac* draws from his Premifes, for he fays : " *Pondera igitur A & P, quæ funt re-* " *ciproce ut Radii in directum pofiti O K, O L, idem* " *pollebunt et fic confiftent in æquilibrio, quæ eft pro-* " *prietas notiffima Libræ, Vectis et Axis in Peritrochio.*" But further, this Property of the Lever, which is here exprefled in general Terms, includes two

Cafes.

Cafes. For the Arms of the Lever may be either perpendicular or oblique to the Directions of the Weights. The firft of thefe Cafes is the fimpleft, and fhould be firft demonftrated: And I do not fee how there can be any room for applying the Refolution of Forces in demonftrating this Cafe, in which no Part of either Weight is loft by oblique Action. But when this Cafe is proved, we have from thence, by the Refolution of Forces, an eafy Way of fhewing, in the fecond Cafe, when the Arms of the Lever are oblique to the Directions of the Weights, that the Weights will counterbalance each other, when they are reciprocally as the perpendicular Diftances of their Lines of Direction from the Center of Motion. From the laft of thefe Cafes, we may deduce an obvious Reafon why the Weight A fhould have the fame Power to turn the Wheel, from whatever Point it hangs in the Line M A; the Truth of which, I am perfuaded, cannot be proved independent of thofe Cafes, and therefore think it ought not to be ufed as a *Poftulatum* in demonftrating the general Property of the Lever.

Mr. *Maclaurin*, in his *View of Newton's Philofophy*, after giving us the Methods which *Archimedes* and *Newton* have ufed for proving the fundamental Property of the Lever, propofes one of his own, which, he fays, appears to be the moft natural one for this Purpofe. However as to his

Method

Method I fhall only obferve, that, from equal Bodies fuftaining each other at equal Diftances from
the *Fulcrum*, he fhews us how to infer that a Body
of one Pound (for Inftance) will fuftain another of
two Pounds at half its Diftance from the *Fulcrum*,
and from thence that it will fuftain one of three
Pounds at a third of its Diftance from the *Fulcrum*:
and thus he goes on deducing, by a kind of In-
duction, what the Proportion is in general between
two Bodies that fuftain each other on the Arms of
a Lever. But this Argument he obferves cannot
be applied when the Arms of the Lever are incom-
menfurable, and therefore it cannot conclude generally, and confequently is imperfect.

Thefe are the Methods of demonftrating the
fundamental Property of the Lever, which are
moft worth taking Notice of ; and, fince they feem
liable to Objections, and the other Methods I have
met with are ftill more exceptionable. I fhall propofe a new Proof of this Property of the Lever,
which appears to me a very fimple one, and depends on a *Poftulatum* that, I believe, will be readily granted.

If a Force be uniformly diffufed over a right
Line, that is, if an equal Part of the Force acts
upon every Point of the Line, and if the whole
Force acts according to one and the fame Plane ;
this

this Force will be fuſtained, and the Line kept in *Æquilibrio*, by a ſingle Force applied to the middle Point of the Line equal to the diffuſed Force, and acting in a contrary Direction.

In order to ſhorten the following Proof, I muſt premiſe by way of *Lemma*, that, if a right Line be divided into two Segments, the Diſtances between the Middle of the whole Line, and the middle Points of the Segments, will be inverſely as the Segments. This is ſelf-evident when the Segments are equal ; and, when they are unequal, then, ſince half of the whole Line is equal to half of the greater and half of the leſſer Segment, it is plain that the Diſtance between the Middle of the whole Line and the Middle of one Segment muſt be equal to half of the other Segment, ſo that theſe Diſtances muſt be to each other inverſely as the Segments, all which appears evident from the Inſpection of Fig. 2.

Let now the Line G H, (Fig. 2) whoſe middle Point is D, be divided into the unequal Segments G L, and L H, whoſe middle Points are C and F, and let two Forces or Weights, A and B, which are to each other as the Segments G L and L H, be applied to their middle Points C and F, and let them act perpendicularly on the Line G H. Then (by the *Lemma*) the Weights A and B will be to each other inverſely as C D, and F D, (the Diſtances

of

of the Points C and F, to which they are applied
from the middle of the whole Line) if then a third
Force or Weight E, equal to the Sum of the
Forces A and B, be applied to the Point D, and
acts on the Line in an oppofite Direction ; I fay
thefe three Forces will fuftain each other, and keep
the Line in *Æquilibrio.* For let us fuppofe the
Force E to be removed and inftead of it another
Force, equal alfo to the Sum of A and B, to be
uniformly diffufed over the whole Line G H, and
to act directly againft the Forces A and B, then
the Part of this Force which acts on the Segment
G L, will be equal to the Force A, and therefore
will be fuftained by it *(Poftulatum)* ; and the other
Part, which is diffufed over the Segment L H, will
be equal to and fuftained by the Force B, fo that
the Forces A and B will fuftain this diffufed Force
and keep the Line in *Æquilibrio.* Let now two
other Forces act alfo on this Line in oppofite Directions, one of them the Force E acting on the
Point D, as it was firft fuppofed to do, and the
other an uniformly diffufed Force equal to E (and
confequently equal to the other diffufed Force),
then thefe two additional Forces will alfo balance
each other, and therefore the *Æquilibrium* will ftill
remain. So that the two Forces A and B, and a
diffufed Force acting on one Side of the Line fuftain the Force E and a diffufed Force acting on the
other Side: but it is manifeft, that in this *Æquili-
bi ium,* the two diffufed Forces acting on oppofite

Sides are perfectly equivalent, and therefore if they are taken away from both Sides, the *Æquilibrium* muſt ſtill remain. Hence it appears that the three Weights or Forces A, B and E, any two of which are (by the Conſtruction) to each other inverſely at their Diſtances from the third, will ſuſtain each other and keep the Line on which they act in *Equilibrio*; which is the firſt and moſt ſimple Caſe of the Property of the Lever; for here the Directions of the Weights are ſuppoſed to be perpendicular to the Line on which they act, and it is evident that, if one of the Points C, D or F be fixed or conſidered as a *Fulcrum*, the Weights acting on the other two Points will continue to ſupport each other. I ſhall not now take the trouble of proving the ſecond Caſe of the Property of the Lever; it is moſt eaſily deduced from the firſt; for when two Weights act on the arms of a Lever in oblique Directions, and are to each other inverſely as the perpendicular Diſtances of their Lines of Direction from the Center of Motion, then, by the reſolution of Forces, it is eaſily proved that the Parts of thoſe Forces which act perpendicularly on the Arms of the Lever, and which only are exerted to turn the Lever, are to each other inverſely as the lengths of thoſe Arms; and therefore by the firſt Caſe they muſt balance each other.

I ſhall now mention ſome well known Truths in Mechanicks, which, I think, cannot be proved otherwiſe than by deducing them from what hath been here demonſtrated.

COROLLARY I. It appears from hence, that the Powers with which any two Forces move or endeavour to move the Arms of a Lever, are as the Rectangles, under Lines proportional to the Forces, and the perpendicular Diſtances of their Lines of Direction from the *Fulcrum.*

COR. II. When therefore two Bodies acting on the Arms of a Lever ſuſtain each other, if one of them be removed farther from the *Fulcrum*, it will preponderate; but if it be brought nearer to the *Fulcrum*, the other Weight will prevail: becauſe the Product to which its Force is proportional will be encreaſed in the firſt Caſe, and diminiſhed in the ſecond.

COR. III. We learn from hence, to find out the Center of Gravity of any two Bodies joined by an inflexible right Line; and to prove that its Definition will agree to one Point only in the Line. For if a Point be taken in the Line ſo that the Diſtances of the Bodies from it may be inverſely as their Weights, that Point will be their Center of Gravity, becauſe, when it is ſuſtained, the Bodies will be in *Æquilibrio.* But if the Line be ſuſtained at

D   any

any other Point, then is the *Fulcrum* removed farther from one Body and brought nearer to the
other than it was when the Bodies balanced each
other ; and therefore, by the preceding Cor. that
Body from which it is removed, or which is on the
fame Side with the Center of Gravity, will defcend. Confequently there is but one Point in
the Line, which being fuftained, the Bodies will
continue in *Æquilibrio,* and therefore but one Point
only can be their Center of Gravity. Hence alfo
it appears, that the Center of Gravity will always
defcend, when it is not directly above or below the
Point by which the Body is fuftained.

I fhall now endeavour to be as concife as poffible
in what I have to fay of the other Mechanic Powers ; having, I fear, been too tedious in my Account of the Lever, which however deferves to
be particularly confidered, fince to it may be reduced the Balance, the Axle and Wheel, and (according to fome Writers) the Pulley.

The Balance I do not confider as a diftinct Ma-
chine, becaufe it is evidently no other than a Le-
ver fitted to the particular Purpofe of comparing
Weights together, and does not ferve for raifing
Weights, or overcoming Refiftances, as the other
Machines do.

What

When a Weight is to be raifed by means of an Axle and Wheel, it is faftened to a Chord that goes round the Axle, and the Power, which is to raife it, is hung to a Chord that goes round the Wheel. If then the Power be to the Weight as the *Radius* of the Axle to the *Radius* of the Wheel, it will juft fupport that Weight ; as will eafily appear from what was proved of the Lever. For the Axle and Wheel may be confidered as a Lever, whofe *Fulcrum* is a Line paffing through the Center of the Wheel and Middle of the Axle, and whofe long and fhort Arms are the *Radii* of the Wheel and Axle which are parallel to the Horizon, and from whofe Extremities the Chords hang perpendicularly. And thus an Axle and Wheel may be looked upon as a kind of perpetual Lever, on whofe Arms the Power and Weight always act perpendicularly, tho' the Lever turns round its *Fulcrum*. And in like Manner when Wheels and Axles move each other by Means of Teeth on their *Peripheries*, fuch a Machine is really, a perpetual compound Lever : and, by confidering it as fuch, we may compute the proportion of any Power to the Weight it is able to fuftain by the help of fuch an Engine. And fince the *Radii* of two contiguous Wheels, whofe Teeth are applied to each other, are as the number of Teeth in each, or inverfely as the number of Revolutions, which they make in the

fame

fame Time; we may, in the computation, inftead of the *Ratio* of thefe *Radii*, put the *Ratio* of the Number of Teeth on each Wheel; or the inverfe *Ratio* of the Number of Revolutions they make in the fame Time.

Some Writers have thought the Nature and Effects of the Pulley might be beft explained by confidering a fixed Pulley as a Lever of the firft, and a moveable Pulley as one of the fecond kind. But tho' the Pulley may bear being confidered in that light; yet, I think, the beft and moft natural Method of explaining its Effects (that is, of computing the Proportion of any Power to the Weight it can fuftain by means of any Syftem of Pulleys) is, by confidering that every moveable Pulley hangs by two Ropes equally ftretched, which muft bear equal Parts of the Weight; and therefore when one and the fame Rope goes round feveral fixed and moveable Pullies, fince all its Parts on each Side of the Pullies are equally ftretched, the whole Weight muft be divided equally amongft all the Ropes by which the moveable Pullies hang. And confequently if the Power which acts on one Rope be equal to the Weight divided by the Number of Ropes, or double the Number of moveable Pullies, that Power muft fuftain the Weight.

Upon this Principle, the Proportion of the Power to the Weight it fuftains by Means of any Syftem

Syſtem of the Pullies, may be computed in a Manner ſo eaſy and natural as muſt be obvious to every common Capacity.

The Proportion which any Power bears to the reſiſting Force it is able to ſuſtain by means of a Wedge, has been laid down differently by different Authors, as they happened to conſider it in particular Caſes. Without examining their ſeveral Opinions, I ſhall endeavour to expreſs this Proportion in one general Propoſition which may extend to the ſeveral Caſes in which the Wedge is applied.

Let the *Æquicrural* Triangle A B C, (Fig. 3.) repreſent a Wedge, the Lines A B and C B will be the Sides of the Wedge, A C its Baſe or Back, and its Height will be the Line P B biſecting the Baſe A C and alſo the vertical Angle A B C. When any two reſiſting Forces act on the Sides of a Wedge in Directions which make equal Angles with the Sides (as they are always ſuppoſed to do) a Power acting perpendicularly at P on the Baſe of the Wedge will keep the reſiſting Forces in *Æquilibrio*, when it is to the Sum of theſe Forces, as the Sine of half the vertical Angle of the Wedge, to the Sine of the Angle which the Directions of the Forces contain with the Sides of the Wedge.

For

For let E and F be two Bodies acting on the Sides of the Wedge, and let them be first supposed to act in the Directions E P and F P perpendicular to the Sides; then since the Power P acts perpendicularly on the Base A C, if these three Forces keep the Wedge in *Æquilibrio* they will be to each other as the Sides of a Triangle to which their Directions are parallel, or (which is the same thing) as the Sides of the Triangle A B C to which their Directions are perpendicular. Therefore the Power P is to the Sum of the resisting Forces which it sustains as A C the Base of the Wedge to the Sum of the Sides, or as P A, half the Base, to A B one of the Sides; but P A is to A B as the Sine of P B A, half the vertical Angle of the Wedge, to the *Radius* which is the Sine of a right Angle, and the Directions of the resisting Forces are supposed in this Case to contain a right Angle with the Sides of the Wedge.

Let now the resisting Bodies E and F be supposed to act on the Wedge in Directions parallel to the Lines D P and O P, which make oblique Angles with its Sides, draw E G and F K perpendicular to those Lines. From what has been proved it appears that the Power P is to the Force with which it is able, by means of the Wedge, to protrude the resisting Bodies in the Directions P E and P F as the Sine of half the vertical Angle
gle

gle to the *Radius*, let this protruding Force be expressed by the Line P E, and let it be resolved into two Forces expressed by the Lines P G and G E, the former of these only will act in opposition to the resisting Bodies, therefore the whole protruding Force of the Power is to the Force with which it acts against the resisting Bodies. P E and P F in the Directions P D and P O as P E to P G or, (because the Triangles E P G and D P E are similar) as P D to P E, that is as the *Radius* to the Sine of the Angle P D E; compounding therefore the *Ratio* of the Sine of half the vertical Angle to the *Radius*, with the *Ratio* of the *Radius* to the Sine of the Angle P D E, the Power P, when the Wedge is kept in *Æquilibrio*, will be to the Force with which it protrudes the resisting Bodies in Directions opposite to those in which they act, as the Sine of half the vertical Angle to the Sine of the Angle P D E or P O F, which the Directions of the resisting Forces contain with the Sides of the Wedge.

Hence, when the Directions in which resisting Bodies act on a Wedge are given, we may easily find two Lines that will express the Proportion between the Resistance and the Power which sustains it by means of the Wedge. For from P the middle Point of the Wedge draw the Line P D meeting one of the Sides, and parallel to the Direction in which the resisting Force acts on that Side,
then

then the Power will be to the Refiftance as P D to P B the Height of the Wedge. For P D and P B are to each other as the Sines of the oppofite Angles, in the Triangle P B D, that is as the Sines of half the vertical Angle, and the Angle which the Direction of the refifting Force contains with the Side of the Wedge.

From what has been demonftrated we may deduce the Proportion of the Power to the Refiftance it is able to fuftain in all the Cafes in which the Wedge is applied. Firft, when in cleaving Timber the Wedge fills the Cleft, then the Refiftance of the Timber acts perpendicularly on the Sides of the Wedge, therefore in this Cafe, when the Power which drives the Wedge, is to the cohefive Force of the Timber, as half the Bafe, to one Side of the Wedge, the Power and Refiftance will be in *Æquilibrio*.

Secondly, when the Wedge does not exactly fill the Clift, which generally happens becaufe the Wood fplits to fome Diftance before the Wedge. Let E L F reprefent a Cleft into which the Wedge A B C is partly driven; as the refifting Force of the Timber muft act on the Wedge in Directions perpendicular to the Sides of the Cleft, draw the Line P D in a Direction perpendicular to E L the Side of the Cleft and meeting the Side of the Wedge in D; then the Power driving the Wedge and

and the Refiftance of the Timber, when they ballance, will be to each other as the Line P D to
P B the Height of the Wedge.

Thirdly, when a Wedge is employed to feparate two Bodies that lie together on an horizontal
Plane, for Inftance two Blocks of Stone; as thefe
Bodies muft recede from each other in horizontal
Directions, their Refiftance muft act on the Wedge
in Lines parallel to its Bafe CA; therefore the Power
which drives the Wedge will ballance the Refiftance when they are to each other as P A half the
Breadth of the Wedge to P B its Height; and then
any additional Force fufficient to overcome the Refiftance arifing from the Friction of the Bodies on
the horizontal Plane will feparate them from each
other.

The inclined Plane is reckoned by fome Writers
among the mechanic Powers; and I think with
Reafon, as it may be ufed with Advantage in
raifing Weights.

Let the Line A B (Fig. 4.) reprefent the length
of an inclined Plane, A D its Height, and the Line
B D we may call its Bafe. Let the circular Body
G E F be fuppofed to reft on the inclined Plane,
and to be kept from falling down it by a String
C S tied to its Center C. Then the Force with

E   which

which this Body ſtretches the String will be to its
whole Weight, as the Sine of A B D the Angle
of Elevation, to the Sine of the Angle which the
String contains with a Line perpendicular to A B
the Length of the Plane. For let the *Radius* C E
be drawn perpendcular to the Horizon, and C F
perpendicular to A B, and from E draw E O parallel to the String and meeting C F in O. Then,
as the Body continues at reſt and is urged by three
Forces, to wit, by its Weight in the Direction
C E, by the Reaction of the Plane in the Direction
F C, and by the Reaction of the String in the Direction E O; the Reaction of the String, or the
Force by which it is ſtretched, is to the Weight
of the Body, as E O to C E: that is, as the Sine
of (the Angle E C O, which is equal to) A B D
the Angle of Elevation, to the Sine of the Angle
E O C, equal to S C O, the Angle which the
String contains with the Line C F perpendicular
to A B, the Length of the Plane.

When therefore the Sting is parallel to the
Length of the Plane, the Force with which it is
ſtretched, or with which the Body tends down the
inclined Plane, is to its whole Weight, as the
Sine of the Angle of Elevation, to the *Radius*,
or as the Height of the Plane to the Length. And
in the ſame Manner it may be ſhewn, that when
the String is parallel to B D, the Baſe of the
Plane, the Force with which it is ſtretched is to

the

the Weight of the Body, as A D to B D, that is, as the Height of the Plane to its Bafe. If we fuppofe the String, which fupports the Body G E F, to be faftened at S, and that a Force, by acting on the Line A D, the Height of the Plane, in a Direction parallel to the Bafe B D, drives the inclined Plane under the Body, and by that Means makes it rife to a Direction parallel to A D. Then, from what was proved in the third Cafe of the Wedge, it will appear, that this Force muft be to the Weight of the Body, as A D to B D, or rather in a Proportion fomewhat greater : if it makes the Plane move on and the Body rife,

From this laft Obfervation we may clearly fhew the Nature and Force of the Screw; a Machine of great Efficacy in raifing Weights or in preffing Bodies clofely together. For if the Triangle A B D be turned round a Cylinder whofe Periphery is equal to B D, then the Length of the inclined Plane B A will raife round the Cylinder in a fpiral Manner; and form what is called the Thread of the Screw, and we may fuppofe it continued in the fame Manner round the Cylinder from one End to the other; and A D the Height of the inclined Plane will be every where the Diftance between two contiguous Threads of this Screw, which is called a Convex Screw. And a Concave Screw may be form-

ed

ed to fit this exactly, if an inclined Plane every way like the former be turned round the Infide of a hollow Cylinder, whofe Periphery is fomewhat larger than that of the other. Let us now fup-pofe the Concave Screw to be fixed, and the Convex one to be fitted into it, and a Weight to be laid on the Top of the Convex Screw: Then, if a Power be applied to the Periphery of this Convex Screw to turn it round, at every Revolution the Weight will be raifed up thro' a Space equal to the Diftance between the two contiguous Threads, that is to the Line A D the Height of the inclined Plane B A; therefore fince this Power, applied to the Periphery, acts in a Direction parallel to B D, it muft be to the Weight it raifes as A D to B D, or as the Diftance between two contiguous Threads, to the Periphery of the Convex Screw.

The Diftance between two contiguous Threads is to be meafured by a Line parallel to the Axle; if we now fuppofe that a Hand-fpike or Handle is inferted into the Bottom of the Convex Screw, and that the Power which turns the Screw is applied to the Extremity of this Handle, which is generally the Cafe; then as the Power is removed farther from the Axis of Motion, its Force will be fo much encreafed (vide what was faid of the Lever, Cor. 1.) and therefore fo much

may

may the Power itfelf be diminifhed. So that the Power, which, acting on the End of a Handle, fuftains a Weight by Means of a Screw, will be to that Weight, as the Diftance between two contiguous Threads of the Screw, to the Periphery defcribed by the End of the Handle. In this Cafe we may confider the Machine as compofed of a Screw and a Lever, or as Sir *Ifaac Newton* expreffeth it, *Cuneus a vecte impulfus.*

Of any two or more of thefe fimple Machines combined together, all other Machines however complicated are compofed. And their Powers and Manner of acting may therefore be explained from the Principles here laid down.

A N

E S S A Y

ON THE

ASCENT OF VAPOURS,

The Formation of

CLOUDS, RAIN and DEW,

And on feveral other

Phænomena of AIR and WATER.

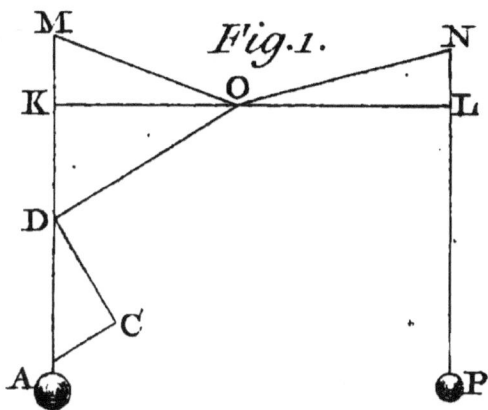

Fig.1.

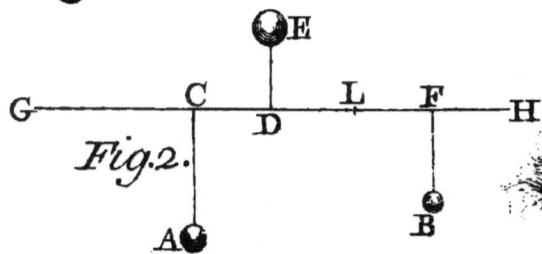

Fig.2.

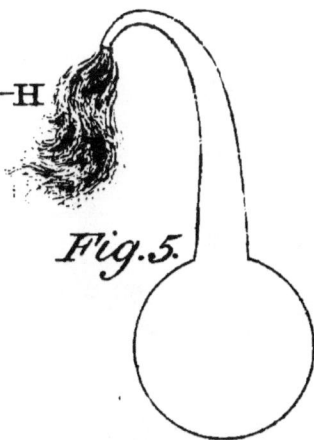

Fig.5.

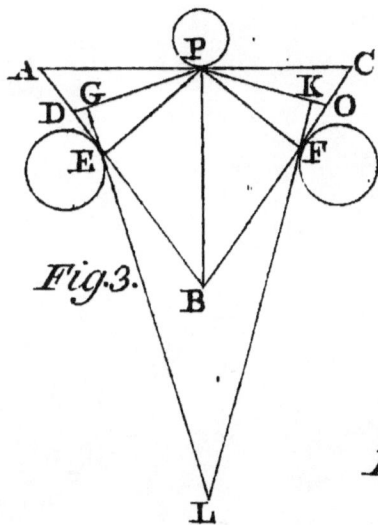

Fig.3.

Fig.4.

ON THE

ASCENT of VAPOURS, &c.*

I Intend in this Essay to give some account of the Nature of Evaporation, the Ascent of Watry Vapours and several other Phanomena of the Atmosphere. In explaining which I shall proceed upon a Principle very different (as far as I can find) from any that has hitherto been used on this

* This Essay was read at a Meeting of the Royal Society on the 9th and 16th of *May*, 1765. communicated in a Letter to the Rev. *Charles Dodgson*, D. D. F. R. S. now Lord Bishop of *Ossory*. *Vide Phil. Transf.* Vol. LIV. To which some Additions and Improvements have been since made by the Author.

F   Occasion;

Occafion; whereby I fhall avoid thofe Objections
which late Writers have made to the former Accounts that have been given us of thefe Phænomena, and perhaps deliver fomething on this Subject that may appear fatisfactory.

In all the Accounts I have met with, Fire, or
Heat and Rarefaction, by which Watry Vapours
are fuppofed to become fpecifically lighter than
Air, are made to be the principal, if not the only
Caufes of their Afcent into the Atmofphere. Doctor *Niewentyt*, and fome others fuppofed, that the
Particles of Fire, by adhering to thofe of Water,
make up *Moleculæ* or fmall Bodies fpecifically
lighter than Air. And Doctor *Halley* thought,
that by the Action of Heat the Particles of Water
are formed into hollow Spherules filled with a
finer Air, highly rarefied, fo as to become fpecifically lighter than the external Air. This laft was
the Opinion moft commonly received, as Doctor
Defaguliers tells us in his Differtation on this Subject (publifhed in *The Philofophical Tranfactions*, in the
Year 1729) in which he examines and refutes the
two former Opinions, and endeavours to eftablifh
his own. He afcribes the Afcent of Aqueous Vapours to their being turned into an Elaftic Steam,
and always rarefied more than the Air by the
Degrees of Heat, to which Bodies are ufually
fubject in the different Seafons of the Year.

This

This Opinion, I find, has been as ill received by subsequent Writers, as the former ones. Mr. *Clare*, in his *Treatise on the Motion of Fluids*, has brought many Objections against it; as Mr. *Rowning* has also done in his *System of Natural Philosophy*, not long since published; who says, that the Cause of the Ascent of Vapours has been much disputed, but not yet determined by Philosophers, and owns that he cannot think of any true Principle of Philosophy upon which it may be accounted for.

I shall not here repeat the Objections made by those Gentlemen, but must beg leave to add the two following, which, among many others that might still be urged, they have not taken Notice of.

First; If Heat was the only Cause of Evaporation, Water in a close Room would evaporate faster than when exposed in a colder Place where there is a constant Current of Air, which is contrary to Experience.

Secondly; The Evaporation of Water is so far from depending on its being rarefied by Heat, that it is carried on even whilst Water is condensed by the Coldness of the Air. For Water is gradually condensed by Cold, 'till the Moment it freezes; and since it evaporates even when frozen

F 2   into

into hard Ice, it muft evaporate in all the leffer Degrees of Cold. Mr. *Boyle* having counterpoifed a Piece of Ice in a Scale, hung it out in a frofty Night, and found next Morning that it loft confiderably of its Weight by Evaporation, " Who " would have thought, fays he, that fo extremely " hard and cold a Body would evaporate fo faft " in the clear Air of a freezing Night?" and fince that Time others have obferved the fame Thing; which Fact feems to be an unanfwerable Objection to all the Accounts in which Rarefaction by Heat is made to be the chief, if not the only Caufe of Evaporation: and therefore we muft have Recourfe to fome other Principle to affift us in accounting for this Phænomenon.

As the Author of Nature does not employ in his Works a greater Variety of Caufes than is abfolutely neceffary, it is the Bufinefs of natural Philofophy to reduce as many Phænomena as may be to fome general well-known Caufe; and this is to be done by comparing the Phænomena together in their feveral Circumftances, in which if they are found to agree, they are then to be confidered as Effects of the fame Kind, and afcribed to the fame Caufe; by which Means, the Caufes, whofe Exiftence is already proved, will be rendered more general, and our Knowledge more extenfive. Now, as the Sufpenfion of the Particles of Water in Air, of Salt in the Waters of the Ocean, and of

other

other heavy Bodies in the Fluids that diffolve them, feem to be Phænomena of the fame Kind, we might reafonably fuppofe, that they arife from the fame Caufe, and that what we call Evaporation is nothing more than a gradual Solution of Water in Air. But that I may not propofe this merely as an *Hypothefis*, I fhall endeavour to prove the Truth of it, by confidering the Nature of Solution in general and comparing its Properties and Effects with thof of Evaporation.

By Solution we underftand, fuch an intimate Union between the Particles of a Body and thofe of a Fluid, that the Whole fhall appear an Homogeneous Mafs, as tranfparent as the Fluid was before fuch Union, and fhall fo continue, 'till fome external Caufe produces a Change. The Nature of Solution has been explained by the Writers on Chymiftry in this Manner ; When the Particles of any Body furrounded by a Fluid are lefs ftrongly attracted by each other than by the Fluid, they muft feparate from each other, and join themfelves to thofe of the Fluid, and remain fufpended therein : Thus various Salts are diffolved in Water, effential Oils in Spirits of Wine, Gold in *Aqua Regia*, Mercury, Silver and other Metals in other acid Spirits ; and indeed it feems to be with great Appearance of Reafon, that the Attraction between the minute Particles of different Bodies (of which we have fo many other Inftances) is affigned

as

as the Caufe of that Union between them, which we experience in Solutions; the chief Properties of which I fhall now mention, fo far as may be neceffary for the Purpofe to which I mean to apply them.

In moft Cafes a diffolving Fluid, or *Menftruum* as the Chymifts call it, will diffolve or take up only a certain Proportion of the Body immerfed, and if then any more of the fame Body be added, it will ~~████████~~ fall to the Bottom, and then the Fluid is faid to be *faturated* with the Body it has diffolved; yet a Fluid which is faturated with one Body may afterwards diffolve others of different Kinds, and keep all their Particles fufpended together.

When any *Menftruum* has entirely diffolved a Body, it will continue as tranfparent as it was before; the Caufe of which may be affigned from what Sir *Ifaac Newton* difcovered by Experiments, *viz.* that the Particles of Bodies muft be of a certain Size or Bignefs to caufe any Reflection or Refraction of the Rays of Light at their Surfaces to which Opacity is owing; whence he gives the Reafon, why fome Bodies are opake and others tranfparent. He alfo obferves, that the moft opake Bodies (fuch as Metals) being diffolved in an acid *Menftruum*, and thereby reduced to their ultimate and fmalleft Particles, do not take away the Tranfparency of the *Menftruum*.

Hence

Hence we may always know how to diſtinguiſh a Solution from a Mixture. For, if a Body be reduced to Powder and thrown into a Fluid that will diſſolve it, and they are then ſhaken ſuddenly together, the Fluid will continue ſomewhat opake, 'till the Solution be effected, or 'till what remains undiſſolved falls to the Bottom; for in this Caſe, the Particles are not at firſt reduced to their ſmall-eſt Size, as they always are in a Solution. I think therefore we may conſider the Tranſparency of an heterogeneous Fluid (or one that contains in it Particles of another Body) as the *Criterion* of a true Solution; and where that is wanting, it is only a Mixture; as when Water and Air appear together in Froth, or in a Cloud, or a thick Miſt, it is only a Mixture of thoſe Bodies, and not a Solution of one in the other.

This much being premiſed concerning the Nature of Solutions in general, I proceed to the Proof of what I propoſed; and in Order to this, I ſhall ſhew that there is a mutual Attraction between Water and Air, the ſame that we obſerve between the Particles of any two Bodies, one of which diſſolves the other. I ſhall then compare in ſeveral Inſtances, the Properties and Effects of common Solutions with thoſe of Evaporation; that from the exact Reſemblance between theſe two Phænomena, it may appear that they are na-

tural

tural Operations or Effects of a like Kind, and therefore to be explained upon the same Principle, or ascribed to the same Cause. Thence I shall shew, how the Ascent of Vapours, and several other Phænomena of the Atmosphere may be accounted for. And lastly, I shall add something on the rising of Steam from boiling Liquors, and shew wherein it differs from common Evaporation.

I am first to prove that there is an Attraction between the Particles of Air and Water. It is well known, that all Water contains a considerable Quantity of Air, that retains its Elasticity by Means of which it may be separated from the Water by boiling and including it in an exhausted Receiver. And it has been proved by Experiments, that Air extricated from Water by boiling, and restored to its usual Density, will occupy a Space greater than that possessed by the Water in which it was contained. Now since it is allowed that the Particles of so heavy a Body as Gold are suspended in *Aqua Regia* by their Attraction towards the Particles of that Fluid, it seems reasonable to suppose, that so light and elastic a Body as Air must be retained under Water by a like Force, without which it would always ascend to the Surface and escape. But that there is really such an attractive

Force

Force between Air and Water, has been fully proved by the following Experiment.

Let an Oil-Flask be filled almoft full with Water, deprived of its Air, as much as may be; let the Mouth of it be then ftopped, until the Neck being inverted is immerfed in a Veffel of Water; a Bubble of Air will then afcend into the upper Part of the Flaſk. When Things have ftood in this Way for fome Days, the Water will be found to have abforbed the whole Bubble of Air (if it was not too large) and entirely filled the Flaſk. But if the Bubble was too large, part of it will be left; for the Water, after fome time, will abforb no more Air, being then fufficiently faturated with it. It is obfervable that a Part of the included Air enters pretty quickly into the Water at firft, but what remains afterwards makes its Way in but very flowly. This Experiment fhews that Water, when deprived of its Air, will again draw the Air gradually into its Pores; juft in the fame Manner as a Lump of dry Sugar will draw up Water into its Pores, which will afcend pretty quickly at firft, but very flowly after fome Time. We have Reafon therefore to conclude, that there is the fame kind of Attraction between Air and Water, that there is between Water and any dry porous Body that will imbibe it.

G As

As Water contains a confiderable Quantity of Air, fo does Air contain a good deal of Water, even when we think it quite pure and dry ; as appears from the Moifture drawn from it by dry Salt of Tartar, in fuch Quantity as to make the Salt become entirely fluid. Now fince the Air is an heterogeneous Fluid containing in it Particles of another Body, and yet retaining a perfect Tranfparency, which is the *Criterion* of a true Solution in other Cafes ; why fhould we not infer from Analogy, that in this Cafe alfo there is a true Solution of Water in Air ?

But the Truth of this will be confirmed by farther comparing the Properties of common Solutions with thofe of Evaporation; which I fhall now do in feveral Inftances.

Firft ; When a Body is immerfed in a Fluid that diffolves it, for Inftance a Lump of Salt in Water, we fee the Salt foon begin to diffolve, and impregnate with its Particles the Water that furrounds it, which will then appear thick and loaded, and if the Water be at Reft the Solution will proceed very flowly ; but if it be ftirred about, the Salt will foon be entirely diffolved. How exactly does this correfpond with what Dr. *Halley* remarked in an Experiment he made on the

Evaporation

Evaporation of Water in a clofe Room? (*Philof.
Tranf.* No. 192.) " The fame Obfervations
" fays he, do likewife fhew an odd Quality in
" the Vapours of Water, which is, that of adhering
" to the Surface that exhales them, which they
" clothe as it were with a Fleece of vapourous
" Air, which once invefting it, the Vapour rifes
" afterwards in much lefs Quantity." Here we
fee, that the Air which lay at reft over the Water
appeared thick and loaded with the aqueous Particles, and then the Evaporation proceeded very
flowly; juft as the Water that lies about the Salt,
appears thick and loaded, and while it continues
at reft, the Salt is diffolved but flowly. He alfo
obferves on the fame Occafion, that Evaporation
is vaftly promoted by a Current of frefh Air paffing over the exhaling Surface : and this I have no
doubt happens for the fame Reafon that Solution
is greatly promoted by Agitation, which continually brings frefh Particles of the Fluid into contact with the Body it diffolves, in the Place of
thofe that have been already faturated. [A]

G 2 Secondly,

[A] This Fleece of vapourous Air that fome times hangs over
Water, is very difcernable when we ftand by the Sea-fide in a
hot calm Day, and is the Caufe of fome odd Appearances.
For the lower Part of the Air, which is then much impregnated with Water, refracts the Rays of the Light more ftrongly
than at other Times, and by this unufual Degree of Refraction,
Houfes

Secondly; Into a Glaſs of clear cold Water throw a Lump of any Salt which is ſoluble in it, and when it has ſtood a little Time, ſhake the Glaſs or ſtir the Water very gently, and the Water which is ſaturated with the Salt will riſe up among the reſt of the Water in curled Wreaths or long *Striæ*, which will render the Water ſome-what opake, cauſing it to refract in different Di-rections the Light of an Object ſeen through it, and will make the Object appear to have a tre-mulous Motion ; this will continue until all Parts of the Water are equally impregnated with the Salt, and then its Tranſparency will be reſtored. As the Parts of the Water which are impregnated with the Salt are of different Denſities from the reſt, while they are mixing together, they muſt occaſion thoſe Refractions and this apparent tre-mulous Motion, which will ceaſe as ſoon as all the Water becomes of the ſame Denſity. The very ſame Appearances will attend the mixing to-gether of any two Fluids of different Denſities, and which will thoroughly incorporate with each other.

Houſes on the Shore at a Diſtance from us appear almoſt as high as Steeples, remote Ships and Iſlands and the extreme Parts of Head-lands or Promontories appear to be raiſed quite out of the Water, and to hang in the Air above its Surface.

In like manner, when Smoke or Steam, iſſuing from the Pipe of a boiling Veſſel, firſt riſes into the Air, it appears in curled Wreaths and renders the Air opake; but as ſoon as it is entirely diſperſed, the Tranſparency is reſtored. Thus alſo in a calm, hot, Sun-ſhine Day, when we look along a moiſt Piece of Ground, the Air and any Object ſeen through it appear to have a tremulous Motion, like that which we obſerve in an Object, ſeen through two Fluids which are mixing together. Now, as the Vapours riſe here in great Abundance and the Air has but little Motion, thoſe Parts of it that are much impregnated with aqueous Particles are mixed gradually with the Air that is drier and of a different Denſity; which will occaſion Refractions of the Light, and that apparent tremulous Motion, juſt now mentioned; and in this Caſe, the Solution of Water in Air (if I may yet venture to call it by that Name) is carried on in a Manner viſible to the Eye, as Solutions are in other Fluids. The ſame tremulous undulating Motion is more obſervable, when we look in warm Weather through a Teleſcope, which magnifies the Vapours floating in the Air: and from this kind of Refraction the twinkling of the Stars ſeems to ariſe; with this Difference only, that the watry refracting Particles in the Day-time are paſſing into a State of Solution, whereas the Vapours already diſſolved are by the Cold of the

Night

Night beginning to precipitate, and return into Particles large enough to caufe Refractions in the Light of the Stars.

Thirdly; Heat promotes, and Cold in fome Meafure ftops or checks both Solution and Eva-poration. Very hot Water will diffolve Salt fooner and in a greater Quantity than cold Water; and if a ftrong Solution of Salt be made in hot Water, the Water when cold will let go fome of the Salt before diffolved, which will fall to the Bottom in fmall Particles or fhoot into Chryftals. Juft fo will Water evaporate fafter in warm than in cold Air; and the aqueous Vapours fufpended in the Air during the Heat of the Day, fall down at Night and form themfelves into Drops of DEW, or if the Night be very cold appear next Morning Chryftalized in a HOAR-FROST. And thus if in a hot Day a Bottle be filled with any very cold Liquor, and expofed to the warm Air, which to us feems very dry, a Dew will be foon formed on the outfide of the Bottle; for the Air about it be-coming cold will let go Part of its Moifture, which will be attracted to the Surface of the Glafs; for the fame Reafon a Dew is formed on the Infide of the Windows of a warm Room which on their Outfide are expofed to the cold Air. Hence alfo we may obferve, that as there cannot be fo conti-nual and copious an Evaporation in cold Weather, the Air will then be generally clearer than it is in hot Weather,

Heat

Heat feems to promote Solution, becaufe it expands Bodies, and thereby enlarges their Pores, and leffens the cohefive Attraction of their Particles; fo that a Body, when hot, will more eafily admit a diffolving Fluid into its Pores, and its Particles not cohering together fo ftrongly, as when cold, will more readily quit each other, and unite themfelves to the Particles of the Fluid by which they are attracted; and for the fame Reafon Heat will alfo promote the Evaporation of Fluids.

But fourthly; The Quantity of a Body diffolved, and of a Fluid evaporated, in a given Time, depends (*cæteris paribus*) on its Quantity of Surface. Thus a Body reduced to Powder is fooner diffolved than when it is in a folid Form; and thus Smoak or Steam (which is Water reduced to very fmall Particles by Heat) is much fooner difperfed and incorporated with Air, than Water in its ufual Form.

Fifthly; Chymifts obferve, that when Sea-Salt, *Sal Ammoniac*, or Nitre, is diffolved in Water, or effential Oils in Spirit of Wine, fome Degree of Cold is produced in the immediate Act of Solution; and the quicker the Solution, the greater is the Cold. By diffolving pounded Ice, or rather Snow (whofe Particles have a greater Surface) in Spirit of Nitre, a Degree of Cold has been produced fo great as to freeze Quick-filver. Cold is likewife produced in the Act of Evaporation. For

if

if Spirit of Wine, or Æther, having the same Temperature with the Air, be rubbed lightly with a Feather over the Ball of a Thermometer, it will sink as the Spirit evaporate; and the quicker they evaporate, the faster will the Thermometer sink; thus I have made Water freeze in a thin Glass merely by the Evaporation of Æther promoted by a Current of Air. Water will likewise produce Cold, if it be used instead of Spirits, provided its Evaporation be promoted by a strong Current of Air. That Cold is produced by the Evaporation of Water appears from the Practice of Sailors, who, in hot Climates, cool their Liquors by wrapping the Vessels in wet Cloths, and hanging them up where they are much exposed to the Wind and Sun, and wetting the Cloths again when they become dry.

This Observation shews a very remarkable Agreement between the Natures of Solution and Evaporation: How the Cold is produced in either Case, I cannot pretend to say; but I must beg leave just to apply this Fact, to account for a Thing which I believe most People have taken Notice of. If we rub Hungary-Water, or any other volatile Spirit over our Hand, it will feel much colder than Water, tho' they be both of the same Temperature, and will both feel equally cold, if we dip our Finger into each. The Reason of which is, that the Spirit evaporating much quicker than the Water, produces thereby a greater Degree of Cold.

Cold. And so Æther, if it be applied in the same Way, will feel colder than any other Spirit, on Account of its more sudden Evaporation.

Sixthly ; It is known, that rectified Spirit of Wine, when purged of Air, will imbibe a large Bubble of Air in a much shorter Time than Water will do, and I have myself experienced the Truth of this, which shews that there is a stronger Attraction, or *affinity* (as the Chymists call it) between Spirit of Wine and Air, than between Water and Air, and since the Spirit evaporates much faster than the Water, I think we may conclude from hence, that the Evaporation of Fluids arises from an attractive Force between their Particles and those of Air. [B] But here it must be observed that the Spirit is not only more strongly attracted by the Air than Water is, but, being also more easily

[B] As Water and Spirit of Wine are in no degree viscid, they may evaporate in Proportion to the Attraction between them and Air. But the Case is very different in such Fluids as are viscid ; for tho' I found that Oil of Olives, when purged of Air, will imbibe a Bubble of Air almost as soon as Water does, yet the Evaporation of Oil, is scarcely (if at all) sensible. The Reason of which must be, that the Attraction between Air and the Oil is not able to overcome the Tenacity of its Particles and separate them from each other, tho' it is sufficient to draw into the Oil the Particles of Air, which have no Attraction towards each other ; just as Water is drawn into a Sponge, tho' the Attraction of the Water is not able to separate the Particles of the Sponge from each other.

H

rarefied

rarefied by Heat, its Particles feem to cohere together more flightly than thofe of Water, and therefore may be more eafily feparated by the Attraction of the Air.

Seventhly ; If into any *Menftruum* we throw a
Body, which it diffolves, and afterwards add another, to which the *Menftruum* has a greater Affinity
than it has to the firft, it will diffolve the fecond
Body, and let go the firft, which will be precipitated and fall to the Bottom. In the very fame
Manner will a Fluid let go the Air it contains,
upon the Addition of another Body to which it
has a greater Affinity than it has to the Air.
Thus if to well rectified Spirit of Wine we add
an equal Quantity of clear Water, thefe Fluids
(which fo readily incorporate) having a greater
Affinity to each other than to the Air they contain, will let go a great Part of that Air, which
will rife to the Top, or adhere in fmall Bubbles to the Sides of the Veffel. This, I think,
fhews that Air is contained in thefe Fluids, in
the fame Manner that the Particles of a Body
are contained in a *Menftruum* that diffolves it ;
and hence I conclude that the Air which is imbibed by any Fluid is, properly fpeaking, *diffolved*
in that Fluid ; and confequently that any Fluid
which evaporates, or is imbibed by the Air, is
alfo, properly fpeaking, *diffolved* in Air. Upon this
Principle we may fay, that Water is drawn out

of

of the Air by dry Salt of Tartar, from its having a greater Affinity to that Salt than to the Air.

I fhould not have been fo tedious in comparing together the Natures of Solution and Evaporation in fo many Inftances, but that it gave me an Opportunity at the fame Time of explaining fome of the Phænomena that I at firft intended to confider; which Explanations I believe will be admitted, if I am right in the main Point I have endeavoured to prove. And really when we confider how exactly Solution and Evaporation agree, in their feveral Appearances, Properties and Effects, I think we muft be convinced that they are natural Operations of the fame Kind, and that what we call Evaporation, is nothing more than a gradual Solution of Water in Air, produced and promoted by the fame Means (to wit) Attraction, Heat, and Motion, by which other Solutions are effected.

I fhall now endeavour to account for feveral Phænomena of the Atmofphere upon this Principle, which will be ftill further confirmed, if it be found to anfwer the Purpofe to which it is applied.

The loweft Part of the Air being preffed by the Weight of the Atmofphere againft the Surface of

the

the Water, and continually rubbing upon it by its Motion, has thereby an Opportunity of attract-ing and diffolving thofe Particles with which it is in contact and feparating them from the reft of the Water. And fince the Caufe of Solution in this Cafe is the ftronger Attraction of the Particles of Water towards the Air, than towards each other, thofe that are already diffolved and taken up, will be ftill further raifed by the Attraction of the dry Air which lies over them, and thus will diffufe themfelves, rifing gradually higher and higher, and thereby leave the loweft Air not fo much fatu-rated, but that it will be ftill able to diffolve and take up frefh Particles of Water. And thus Ice or Snow will evaporate as well as Water, its Par-ticles being attracted and diffolved by the Air, which is ftrongly preffed againft its Surface; for tho' Heat promotes both Solution and Evaporation, yet we do not find that in either Cafe any fenfible Degree of it abfolutely neceffary. [c]

In this Manner will AQUEOUS VAPOURS afcend flowly into the Atmofphere, even when we fuppofe

[c] Water by freezing is deprived of its Air, which we fee gathered into Bubbles through the Ice, therefore the Subftance of the Ice being deprived of Air, will attract the external Air more ftrongly than common Water does, which is faturated with Air. And on this Account, I fhould think it probable, that Ice, notwithftanding its Hardnefs, will evaporate almoft as faft as common Water.

the

the Air almoſt at reſt, for I believe it is never perfectly ſo. . But the Solution of Water in Air, and
the Aſcent of Vapours, is greatly promoted by
the Motion of the Winds, which bring freſh and
drier Air into the Place of that, which may be already ſaturated and loaded with Moiſture, carrying it, together with its Moiſture, into the higher
Parts of the Atmoſphere and diſperſing it into
all Quarters.

If we ſhould now ſuppoſe the Atmoſphere to remain always of the ſame Temperature as to Heat
and Cold, and to have always the ſame Denſity ;
when it was once ſaturated with Water, all Evaporation would ceaſe, and the Vapours already raiſed
would always remain ſuſpended ; for a Fluid, while
it remains of the ſame Temperature and Denſity,
will never let go the Particles of a Body that it
has diſſolved: We muſt therefore conſider what
are the Cauſes which occaſion the Air ſometimes
to part with the Water it has diſſolved, and
which thereby keep up a continual Circulation of
Vapours ; and theſe I ſhall ſhew to be the frequent
Viciſſitudes of Heat and Cold, Condenſation and
Rarefaction, to which the Atmoſphere is ſubject.

As

As to the Effects of Heat and Cold, I have already shewn that the former promotes, and the latter checks or in some Measure hinders Evaporation as well as other Solutions ; of which I gave an Instance in the Vapours that are suspended in the Heat of the Day, and by the Cold of the Night are precipitated and suffered to coalesce into Drops of Dew. From the Snow that lies so long on the Tops of the Mountains, and from the Experience of those who have passed over them, we find that the higher Parts of the Atmosphere are much colder than the lower. Now tho' Vapours are first raised, and abound most in the lower Parts of the Atmosphere, yet they cannot there form themselves into Clouds, because the Heat that helped to dissolve them, helps also to keep them dissolved. But when they are carried by the Winds into the higher Parts, where the same Heat is wanting, the cold Air will not be able to keep dissolved all that are carried up, but must suffer some of them to coalesce into small Particles, which slightly attracting each other and being intermixed with Air will form CLOUDS, having the very same Appearance with Steam or Smoke, which also consists of small Particles of Water *mixed* with Air and not yet *dissolved* in it. These Clouds when first formed will remain suspended, though they consist of Water, as well as

Air ;

Air; becaufe the Weight of their Particles will not be able to overcome the Refiftance they muft meet with in defcending through the Air. For when Bodies are diminifhed, their Quantities of Matter, to which their Weights are proportional, decreafe fafter, or in a greater *Ratio*, than their Surfaces to which the Refiftance they meet with is proportional, and therefore in very fmall Particles, this refiftance may become greater than their Weight. The different Heights at which Clouds are formed, depends on the Quantity of Vapours carried up, and the Degrees of Heat in the upper Parts of the Atmofphere; for the Vapours may always afcend 'till they meet with Air fo cold or fo thin that it is not able to keep diffolved all that are carried up; hence Clouds are generally higher in Summer than in Winter. When Clouds are much increafed by a continual Addition of Vapours, and their Particles are driven clofe together by the Force of the Winds, they will run into Drops heavy enough to fall down in RAIN. Sometimes the Clouds are frozen before their Particles are gathered into Drops, and then fmall Pieces of them, being condenfed and made heavier by the Cold, fall down in thin Flakes of SNOW, which appear to be Fragments of a frozen Cloud; but if the Particles be formed into Drops, before they are frozen, they become HAIL-STONES.

When

When the Air is replete with Vapours, and a cold Breeze springs up, which it often does from the Sea, the Solution of thefe Vapours is checked, and Clouds are formed in the lower Parts of the Atmofphere, and compofe what we call a Mist or Fog. This generally happens in a cold Morning, but when the Sun has been up for fome time, the warm Air again diffolves thofe watery Particles, and it frequently clears up. In a hot Summer's Day the Air lying over wet Marfhy Ground is copioufly filled with aqueous Vapours, but the Air growing cooler after Sun-fet, will not be able to keep all thofe Vapours diffolved, but muft let fome Part of them unite quickly into very fmall vifible Particles, and form thofe Mifts which appear to rife from Marfhy Grounds in a Summer's Evening. The Vapours near the Ground being more denfe and copious, will be firft affefted by the Cold, and afterwards thofe that are thinner and higher up, fo that the Mift will be low at firft, but will encreafe in Height afterwards. But befides, thefe Grounds and the Water they contain will acquire fuch a Heat from the Sun that they may retain it for fome time, and communicate it to the contiguous Air, fo that the Vapours may continue to rife for fome time after Sun-fet, and will become vifible when they get up a little Way into the cooler Air. After a warm and unclouded Day in

Summer

Summer there falls abundance of Dew, and the Air fcarce recovers its clearnefs 'till towards Morning, when it is pretty much cooled ; but on the firft Return of Heat, at Sun-rife or a little before it, the Water, which is then plentifully fpread over the Ground and the Leaves of Trees and Plants in very fmall Drops, begins again to diffolve, and while it is diffolving occafions that HAZINESS fo obfervable in a hot Summer's Morning about Sunrife and for fome time after. Here it may be proper to obferve, that when the Particles of Water are of a certain Size, they will render the Air equally opake, whether they are paffing into a State of Solution, or returning from it.

Thofe cold thick Morning Fogs I mentioned juft now are often attended with a very light fmall Rain ; for the Vapours are then returning faft from a State of Solution, and we fee the Drops at their firft Formation, and they are fuch as we generally meet with in paffing over high Mountains. So that it feems the Drops of Rain are very fmall when firft formed in the Clouds ; but being driven about by the Motion of the Air in their Defcent, fome of them will probably touch each other and run into a Drop of a larger Size, and the farther they have to fall, the more will their Size be encreafed before they come to the Ground. And for this Reafon, the Drops which fall from the higher Clouds in Summer are found

I

to be generally larger than they are in Winter, when the Clouds are low. It has been likewife obferved that the Drops of Rain are remarkably large that fall in fudden Thunder-Showers; of which the Reafon may be, that the Lightning burfting from a Cloud and expanding itfelf greatly, will fuddenly remove the Air from its Place, which Air muft therefore return to its Place with great Violence, and thereby the watery Particles in the Clouds will be ftrongly agitated and driven againft each other, by which Means they will form themfelves into larger Drops than at other Times. Or perhaps it may be faid, that when a Cloud is filled with Lightning, which is the fame as the electric Matter, the watery Particles like other electrified Bodies, will repel each other, but being fuddenly deprived of this repelling Matter, will by their mutual Attraction come together again with fome Velocity, and therefore will run into Drops larger than ufual.

When the Wind blows from the South, it is generally warm and comes replete with aqueous Vapours which it has diffolved, but coming into a colder Climate it cannot there keep the fame Quantity of Vapours diffolved that it did before, and confequently muft part with fome of them and let them precipitate; and therefore Southerly Winds generally bring us Rain. On the other Hand,

Hand, when the Wind blows from the North, or any Point near it, as it is very cold it cannot have diffolved a great deal of aqueous Vapours where it came from, and therefore coming into a warmer Climate it is ready to diffolve more. And on this Account thefe Winds, if they continue long, are found to be very dry and parching, and are generally attended with fair Weather.

Thefe feem to be the Effects of Heat and Cold, as far as the different Temperatures of the Air will occafion it to diffolve and take up, or let go and precipitate the aqueous Vapours, in confequence of which we fometimes perceive Changes of the Weather, even when there is no Change in the Height of the Barometer.

But Condenfation and Rarefaction will alfo have the like Effects in promoting the Solution of Water in Air, or in occafioning fome Part of what has been diffolved to return again into Water and precipitate. It feems reafonable to fuppofe, that denfe Air in which the Particles lie very near each other, will be better able to diffolve and keep fufpended a Quantity of Water, than the fame Air when diffufed through a greater Space. And that this is really fo, we have an experimental Proof. For when a Receiver is partly exhaufted, we fee the rarefied Air begin to let go the Water

it

it contained, wh   athering into ſmall Particles
appears like Stea   Smoke falling to the Bottom.
In order to prov   e ſame thing by other Experiments, when a   ͐ Water or rather of Spirit
of Wine (which ɛ   . ᷊ faſter) had ſtood for
ſome time in a cloɩ   ᷊iver full of Air, I
rarefied this Air ſuddenly.   ᷊tting it ruſh into
another Receiver that was ɛ   ᷊d, and immediately the Vapour that was ɑ   ᷊ſpended gathered into ſmall Particles and tɩ   in a very
viſible Shower. I alſo took from ɩ.   ᷊ ᷊ᴐump a
large exhauſted Receiver 20 Inches loɩ.   ing at
the Bottom a Braſs Plate, with a Stop-ɕ   ᷊ the
Middle of it, when the Stop-cock waᴕ   ᷊ ᷊ᴄed,
the external Air ruſhing in violently, aɩᴄ   ing
much rarefied, let go the Water it containᴄ   ᷊d
threw it againſt the other End of the Re   r᷊
where it ſtuck on the Glaſs, and covered i   ᷊᷊
a thin Dew, which I found to encreaſe unti
Receiver was almoſt full of Air,

Theſe Experiments prove, that Air when ra
fied, cannot keep as much Water diſſolved as .
does in a more condenſed State. And hence we
muſt conclude, that when the Atmoſphere is ſaturated with Water, and changes from a denſer
to a rarer State, the higher and colder Parts of it
eſpecially will begin to let go ſome of the Water
before diſſolved; which will form new Clouds or
add to the Size or Number of the Particles before
formed,

formed, and thereby render them more apt to fall down in Rain. On the contrary, when the Atmofphere changes from a rarer to a denfer State, it will then be able to ftop the Precipitation of the Water and again diffolve in the Whole, or in Part, fome of thofe Clouds that were formed before, and confequently will render their Particles lefs apt to run into Drops and fall down in Rain. And thus we generally find by Experience, that the rarefied and condenfed States of the Atmofphere are refpectively attended with Rain, or fair Weather. Though this does not happen at all times, for the Air, tho' rarefied, may not then abound much with aqueous Vapours, having already parted with a good deal of them. So likewife when the Air is denfe and heavy it may then be much loaded with aqueous Vapours, which will encreafe its Weight, (and indeed it muft be fo after a long continuance of fair Weather) and we may then have Rain even before we can perceive by the Barometer, that the Atmofphere changes to a rarer State. [D]

Upon

[D] The Vapours raifed into the Atmofphere will certainly add fomewhat to its Weight, but the Difference in the Quantity of Water contained in the Air at one time and at another cannot make any confiderable Change in its Weight. For the Quantity of Rain has been accurately meafured that falls (communibus annis) in feveral Parts of Europe, and by taking thefe Quantities

at

Upon this Principle, I think we may account for the Changes of the Weather, which ufually attend the rifing and falling of the Mercury in the Barometer, better than by faying, that when the Air grows rarer and lighter, it cannot by the Laws of Hydroftaticks fo well fupport the Clouds and, Vapours, and therefore muft permit them to fall down in Drops of Rain. For when the Air grows rarer, altho' the Clouds will defcend into a lower and denfer Part of it, yet they will be there fupported, and I do not fee why their Particles fhould be more apt to run into Drops there, than when they were higher up, unlefs they received fome Addition from the Water depofited among them by the rarefied Air, in the Manner I

at a Medium, I find that in any one Place there will generally fall, one Year with another, as much Rain as would amount altogether to the Height of 28 Inches, which is equivalent in Weight to two Inches of Mercury; if therefore we were to fuppofe this whole Quantity of Rain to be fufpended in the Air at one Time, and then to fall before any more Vapours were taken up, the Mercury in the Barometer would, on that Account, fall two Inches. But we cannot make fuch a Suppofition, for the Rain falls in fmall Quantities and at different Times, and the aqueous Vapours are again taken up into the Air immediately; fo that the Difference in the Quantity of Water fuftained in the Air, at one Time more than at another, can add by its Weight but very little to the Height of the Mercury in the Barometer, probably not fo much as the tenth Part of an Inch.

have

have juſt now mentioned. For ſince the Air is rarefied gradually, the Clouds can deſcend but very ſlowly, and therefore their Particles will not be ſo much preſſed together by the Reſiſtance they meet with in their Deſcent, as they generally are by the Winds which blow upon them.

When the Atmoſphere is ſaturated with Water, and grows colder and rarer than it was before, we ſhall then perceive the lower Air begin to part with ſome of the Water it contains, which will fall inſenſibly to the Ground, or adhere to the Walls of Houſes, or other Bodies expoſed to it, and make them become damp or wet. And if the Moiſture ſettles on the ſmooth Surfaces of cold Bodies, ſuch as Marble or other Stones, whoſe Pores cannot imbibe it, it will cover them with a kind of Dew, and then thoſe Bodies are vulgarly ſaid to SWEAT. At this time the Hygrometer being affected by the Moiſture will point to *WET*, and as we perceive from thence, that the Air is diſpoſed to part with the Water it contains, we may generally expect Rain. But when the Air again grows warm or denſe, it will be able again to diſſolve and take up the Water it before depoſited, and the Moiſture on the Bodies expoſed to it will diſappear, the Hygrometer will point to *D R Y*, and we may then promiſe ourſelves fair Weather.

I obſerved

I obferved before * that if a Bottle be filled with a very cold Liquor and expofed to warm Air, a Dew will foon be formed on its Surface, by the Moifture which the cooled Air depofites. Now if we fuppofe this Body ftill to retain the fame Degree of Cold whilft the Air paffes over it, the Dew on its Surface will continually encreafe and run down its Sides in fmall Streams of Water. This feems to be exactly the Cafe of Mountains whofe Tops reach into the colder Parts of the Atmofphere, and which therefore are themfelves colder than the Air in general. For when the Wind blows the lower Parts of the Atmofphere (which are the warmeft and moft replete with Vapours) againft the Sides of the Mountains, it being there ftopped in its Courfe, muft neceffarily afcend and pafs over their Tops; this Air will therefore be confiderably cooled in its Progrefs up the Sides and over the Tops of the Mountains, and confequently muft let go a great Part of the watery Vapours it contains; which will be precipitated in Dew and Moifture, upon the Surface of the Mountains where it will fink into the earthy Parts, or infinuate itfelf into the Chinks and Crevices of Rocks, and being there collected will afterwards break out in SPRINGS and FOUNTAINS, and become the Source of RIVERS, which are known to take their Rife in mountainous Countries. And on this Account

* Page 46.

count we might have fmall Springs and Rivers near Mountains tho' there were neither Clouds nor Rain. But the Moifture which the Air ufually depofits on the Mountains muft be confiderably encreafed by the Clouds which are driven againft them, and accumulated by the Winds, for their Particles being then preffed together will run into fmall Drops of Rain. Befides, it is well known that Mountains gather and retain the Clouds about them by their Attraction, in confequence of which we often fee fome Clouds continue at reft on the Mountains, whilft the others are carried on gently by the Wind. Hence it is that Countries in the Neighbourhood of high Mountains are the moft fubject to frequent Rains.

Thus I have fhewn how the Afcent of aqueous Vapours and their conftant Circulation, by precipitating again in Moifture and Drops of Rain, will arife from the diffolving Power of the Air, influenced by the Viciffitudes of Heat and Cold, Condenfation and Rarefaction; which Caufes, as they take Place in different Degrees, will occafion thofe various States of the Atmofphere in refpect to Drynefs or Moifture which we experience in the feveral Changes of the Weather. To which the Winds contribute very much by heating or cooling, condenfing or rarefying the different Parts of the Atmofphere, and by promoting the Solution of Water in Air, as they mix thofe

K　　　　　　　Fluids

Fluids together, or (when the Air is already faturated with aqueous Vapours,) by preffing together the Particles in the Clouds, and thereby caufing them to run into Drops.

If we may thus, from the known Properties of Solution, account in a fatisfactory Manner for the Afcent and Circulation of aqueous Vapours, and the feveral Phænomena of the Atmofphere arifing from thence; it muft be a great Confirmation of the Arguments brought to prove that Evaporation is only a particular Species of Solution; and therefore that they both proceed from the fame Caufe, *viz.* the Attraction that obtains between the minute Particles of different Bodies, which is the Means of carrying on fo many other Operations of Nature.

And indeed upon this principle, Air feems better fitted to be a general *Solvent* than any Fluid we know of; becaufe its Particles, not attracting each other, are more at liberty to unite themfelves to the minute Particles of fuch Bodies as they do attract. And accordingly we find the Atmofphere contains in it Matter of all kinds. The odoriferous Particles of Bodies feem to be ftrongly attracted by the Air, as they are fo very readily difperfed thro' it; and Camphor, which is a very light Volatile

latile Body, may be entirely diffolved in Air without leaving any Remainder. The Air abounds with Vitriolic and other Acids, as is plain from the rufting of Iron expofed to it. It abounds alfo with fulphurous, nitrous, and other inflammable Particles, as appears by the frequent Meteors kindled in it. For we have many Subftances, fuch as ftrong Acids and effential Oils, which being thrown together will unite with fuch Violence as fuddenly to burft into a Flame, and therefore when the Particles of thofe Bodies, floating promifcuoufly in the Air, happen to come together in a fufficient Quantity by their mutual Attraction (which we know is very ftrong) they muft kindle into a Flame, and if many Particles of the inflammable Kind lie contiguous, the Fire will run in a Train and form, what we call, fhooting Stars, and other blazing Meteors. In fhort, the Atmofphere may be confidered as a Chaos containing Particles of all forts of Bodies; and as the great Inftrument of Nature for keeping up a general Circulation of Matter; and by which not only Water is every where difperfed, but oftentimes the Eggs of Infects and the Seeds of Plants are conveyed from Place to Place, both which have been found in Rain-water, on examining it carefully juft after it had fallen; and indeed we fometimes find Infects and Plants in fome Places where their Appearance cannot well be accounted

K 2   for,

for, otherwife than by fuppofing their Eggs and Seeds to be conveyed thither by the Air.

I fhall now mention two other Inftances in which this diffolving Power of the Air produces Effects of the utmoft Importance. Dr. *Boerhaave*, fpeaking of that Power or Quality of Air, which makes it neceffary for the Prefervation of Animal Life ; calls it a certain hidden Virtue, not to be accounted for from any of the Properties of Air then difcovered. Perhaps we may be led to fome Knowledge of it, by confidering on what account Air may become unfit for Refpiration by paffing two or three times thro' the Lungs of an Animal, for we find that an Animal inclofed in fuch Air will foon expire. I think we may be fure that one Purpofe, at leaft, for which Air was defigned is, the carrying off that Moifture and other perfpirable Matter which conftantly exhales from the Lungs, for this we know it actually does. Now as Air lofes nothing of its Elafticity by paffing thro' the Lungs, an Animal might ftill continue to breathe the fame Air, and it would ftill continue fit for all fuch Purpofes in the Animal Oeconomy as may be anfwered by the alternate Expanfion and Contraction of the Lungs in Refpiration. But this Air muft in a fhort Time become faturated with that Moifture and other perfpirable Matter which it meets with

in

in the Lungs, and muft then lofe its Power of diffolving and carrying off any more of that kind of
Matter; which Nature intends fhould be conftantly
difcharged, and which will therefore continually
encreafe and thereby opprefs the Lungs, heat the
Blood, or produce fuch other noxious Effects as
are more immediately fatal than thofe arifing from
the ftoppage of external Perfpiration. So that an
Animal inclofed in fuch Air cannot live long, and
will perhaps die fomewhat in the fame Manner as
if it had been drowned. [ε] Whether the Air we
breathe may depofite, in our Lungs, any kind of
Matter neceffary to the Support of Life, I cannot
pretend to judge, nor is it my Defign to enquire;
what has been faid fhews the neceffity of frefh Air
in Refpiration, and by what Property it is adapted
to anfwer one very important Purpofe, and alfo
how Air may foon become unfit for that Purpofe.
But here I will venture to afk, whether it is not
probable, that, in the conftant and quick Evaporation of Moifture from the Lungs, fome Degree of
Cold may be produced, as in other Evaporations,

which

[ε] As Air even when incorporated with Water retains its
Elafticity, I took it for granted that it would not become lefs
elaftic by paffing thro' the Lungs of an Animal. But finding
that the contrary Opinion was held by fome, who fuppofed
that Air, having paffed thro' the Lungs of an Animal, became
unfit for Refpiration by lofing its Elafticity, I refolved to try
how the Fact was by the following Experiment. In a Receiver

eight

which, together with the fresh Air taken in, may
serve to cool the Lungs and the Blood passing thro'
them? We may see from hence that moist
Air

eight Inches in Diameter and twelve Inches high, having under
it a Piece of oiled Leather, I included a pretty large Chicken,
and tied the Receiver close down to the Table; thro' a Hole
in the Top of the Receiver went a Glass Tube, open at both
Ends, cemented round the Hole with Wax; the lower End was
immersed in Water (tinged blue) which stood in a Glass under
the Receiver.

In about an Hour after the Chicken was included it grew
much distressed, gaped wide and breathed with great difficulty,
and in half an Hour more it seemed almost ready to expire;
the Inside of the Receiver was then covered with Moisture
which in some Places ran down in Drops.

Now if the included Air had lost any of its Elasticity by
passing thro' the Lungs of this Animal, it could not have pressed
so strongly on the Water in the Glass as it did at first, and
then the external Air would have pressed thro' the Tube, and
appeared coming up through the Water in Bubbles. But no
such Thing happened, for as soon as the Receiver was tied down,
the Water in the Tube rose about one-fifth of an Inch above the
Water in the Glass, and so continued during the whole Time of
the Experiment, except that it rose and fell near one-tenth of an
Inch every time the Chicken breathed; and these Vibrations of
the Water in the Tube I observed grew slower, and moved thro'
a greater Space towards the latter End of the Time; which
shewed that the Chicken then took in more Air every Time it
breathed, than it did at first, endeavouring thereby to throw
off the Moisture which then oppressed its Lungs. After Things
had stood thus above an Hour and a Half, those who saw the
Experiment were convinced that the included Air had not lost
any of its Elasticity, tho' grown quite unfit for Respiration, the
Animal being ready to expire in it.

Air muſt be very unwholeſome by its not ſufficiently promoting the neceſſary Perſpiration both
internal and external.

Air is not leſs neceſſary for the Support of Fire
than of animal Life; for Fire will not long continue
to burn without a Circulation of Air. Now I ſuppoſe this happens, not from its adding any thing to
the *Pabulum* of Fire, (for Fire ſeems to be otherwiſe
ſufficiently provided with *Pabulum*) but rather on
this Account; that the Air immediately about a Body
on Fire is heated and made ſpecifically lighter than
the Air at ſome Diſtance from it; This hot Air
muſt therefore aſcend and carry with it all thoſe
minute Particles of different kinds which are
thrown off from the burning Body, and which
would otherwiſe reſt upon its Surface, and thereby
clog and ſtop the ſubtile Vibrations of the burning
Matter, in which the Nature of Fire partly conſiſts. If therefore Fire be confined in a cloſe
Place, where there can be no Circulation of freſh
Air, the Air about it, being ſoon ſaturated with
the Particles ariſing from the burning Matter, will
not be able to take up any more of them, and
therefore the Fire muſt go out, ſmothered as it were
with ſuch Particles as are no longer combuſtible.
And hence it is that Fire burns faſter when Air is
ſtrongly blown upon it, for then the Aſhes are
carried off as faſt as they are formed on the Surface of the burning Body, and thereby the Particles

cles that have juft taken Fire are kept quite free from any thing that can impede and clog their vibratory Motion. The Air in this Cafe will alfo fpread the Fire quickly thro' the Fuel by blowing the Particles that are already kindled among thofe that are not; and perhaps the Motion of the Air in this Cafe may promote the fubtile Vibrations in the burning Matter by which the Fire is propagated thro' its Parts.

To this general Obfervation, that Air is neceffary for the Support of Fire, we muft admit one Exception; for Nitre will burn in a clofe Veffel or in *Vacuo*. The Caufe of this fingular Phænomenon I fhall endeavour to affign from what has been faid. Nitre, when fet on Fire, burns with more Rapidity and Violence than any Body we know of, it's burning is a kind of Explofion and produces a very fierce and elaftic Flame, for which Reafon it is a neceffary Ingredient in Gun-powder, *Pulvis fulminans*, and all other fulminating Compounds. When therefore a Piece of Nitre takes Fire, its elaftic Flame drives off the Fumes and Vapours (with which the Air in the Veffel may be then faturated) and defends the burning Matter, fo that they cannot fettle upon it and extinguifh it, as they do other Bodies that burn flowly and without any Explofion. And on this Account Nitre, and other inflammable Matter mixed with it, will burn in clofe Veffels or even in *Vacuo*. This will further appear from confidering the Manner in which Nitre

firft

firſt takes Fire, and the Reaſon of its exploding Quality. Nitre will not burn by itſelf tho' melted and made red hot, but when it comes in Contact with any Body actually on Fire, and which therefore contains an inflammable Matter, or (as it is called) the *Phlogiſton*, it burſts into a Flame. Here the Chymiſts ſay, that the acid Spirit of the Nitre unites ſo rapidly with the *Phlogiſton*, which is detached from the burning Matter, that by the Violence of their Congreſs they both vaniſh together in a Flame. And they prove this to be ſo, by throwing ſtrong Acid of Nitre on any thick eſſential Oil, which conſiſts almoſt wholly of the *Phlogiſton*, for then the Mixture will ſuddenly burſt into a Flame with a violent Exploſion. Therefore ſo long as Nitre and the inflammable Matter are thus in Contact, no Fumes or Vapours floating about them can prevent that rapid Union between their Parts which muſt neceſſarily make them continue to burn. The Air, which is produced from burning Nitre may poſſibly add to the Elaſticity of its Flame. But I do not think it probable that this Air can contribute much to keep a large Quantity of Nitre burning ſo long as it will do in a cloſe Veſſel.

Having thus ſhewn by what Property Air produces the Evaporation of Fluids and ſeveral other Effects, I come now to treat of thoſe Vapours that are raiſed merely by Heat. Al-

L

though

though the Particles of Fluids in common Evaporation are raifed into the Atmofphere by the attracting and diffolving Power of the Air, yet in fome particular Cafes Vapours will rife into the Air on another Account. For in fome Places the Earth often fends forth hot elaftic Vapours that rife into the Air by Means of their Elafticity, and carry up with them Mineral and Foffile Particles of different kinds. Fermentation generates elaftic Vapours which expand themfelves into the Air. And the Particles of Water and other Fluids, when fufficiently heated, acquire a repelling Force which feparates them from the Surface, and throws them upwards into the Air. But all thefe Vapours foon lofe that Elafticity by which they were at firft raifed, and they muft then be retained and kept fufpended in the Air by the fame Power that keeps up all the Vapours that rife without any Elafticity in common Evaporation.

That the Particles of Steam which rife from hot Water are endued with a repelling Force appears plainly when Water is boiled in a clofe Veffel, for then the Steam becomes fo exceedingly elaftic that, unlefs proper Care be taken, it will burft the ftrongeft Veffel. In this Cafe the boiling Water, being ftrongly preffed by the Force of the included Steam, conceives a much greater Heat than it will ever do in an open Veffel; for even when Water is boiled in the open Air it is fome-

what

what hotter when the Atmofphere is heavy, than
when it is light, which fhews that Preffure upon
boiling Water encreafes its Heat; the Reafon of
which we may perhaps fee prefently. But the
moft remarkable Phænomenon that attends the
boiling of Water, is the large Bubbles which continue to rife from the Bottom fo long as the Water
boils, and long after all the Air is driven out of it,
of the Nature of which there have been various
Opinions. Doctor *Boerhaave*, in his *Elements of
Chymiftry*, proves by feveral Arguments, that thefe
Bubbles do not arife from Air, and with regard
to their Production, he feems to be of the fame
Opinion with *Stairs* (to whofe Work he refers) that
they arife from fome active Fires refiding in the
Water. *Marriotte*, whom he alfo mentions on
this Occafion, calls thefe Bubbles *Fulminations*, and
fuppofes that they may proceed from fome kind of
faline Particles contained in the Water, which,
being heated, act in the fame Manner that the
Aurum fulminans does when melted. It has been
alfo a received Opinion that thefe Bubbles are occafioned by fome fubtile elaftic Fluid tranfmitted
from the Fire through the Bottom of the Veffel.
However I conceive that a Fluid fo fubtile as to
pafs thro' the Bottom of the Veffel, would pafs
alfo thro' the Water fo eafily as not to difturb it;
and therefore I have for fome time fufpected, that
thefe Bubbles are formed only by an elaftic Steam
in the Manner I fhall now defcribe. The Particles

cn the Surface of the Water, long before it boils, will, by Means of the repelling Force which the Heat introduces among them, rife in Steam and will infinuate themfelves into the Air which yields eafily to them; but thofe Particles that are preffed againft the Bottom, by the Weight of the Atmof-phere, and of the incumbent Water, will require a greater Degree of Heat to render them fo elaftic that they fhall be able to overcome this Preffure, and expand themfelves into a greater Space. Now fince Heat expands Water and makes its Particles repel each other, according to its differ-ent Degrees, we muft fuppofe that thefe Particles, from their being in contact with the Bottom of the Veffel, will at length acquire fuch a Degree of Heat as will give them a repelling Force fufficient to overcome the Preffure they fuftain, and to ex-pand them fuddenly into thofe large Bubbles that afcend thro' the Water when it boils vio-lently.

I have lately made fome Obfervations and Ex-periments which feem to confirm this Opinion. Thefe Bubbles which afcend from the Bottom, I obferved, always grow lefs in their Progrefs up-wards, and thofe fmall Bubbles, that adhere to the Bottom for fome time before they afcend, often difappear entirely before they reach the Surface, which fhews that when the Matter they contain,

or

or any Part of it, lofes the Heat it had at firft, it
is again turned into Water.

When Water that has juft boiled, or is even
confiderably lefs hot than boiling Water, is pour-
ed into a Glafs and fet under the Receiver of an
Air-Pump, and the Air is almoft drawn out, the
Water will boil more violently than it does on the
Fire, the Bubbles breaking out from all Parts of
it. In this Cafe, no fubtile Fluid can be fuppofed to rife thro' the Bottom of the Veffel, but
the Heat which the Water retains will then give
its Particles an elaftic Force fufficient to overcome
the Preffure of what little Air remains in the Receiver, and will expand them into Bubbles. And
that thefe Bubbles are compofed of Steam appears
plainly from this Experiment, for as foon as they
begin to afcend the Receiver is filled with Steam,
which being condenfed by the Cold runs plentifully down its Sides in Water. From hence
we may fee the Reafon why Water in *Vacuo* boils
with a very fmall Degree of Heat.

After a Veffel of Water had boiled till all the
Air-Bubbles were driven out of it, I turned upon
its Mouth a large Glafs that lay under the Water;
the Bubbles, that afcended under the Glafs, re-
mained in the upper Part of it, and forced out the
Water it before contained, and then the elaftic

Matter

Matter in the Glaſs overturned it, and aſcended to the Top in one large Bubble, upon which the Steam on the Surface was much encreaſed. Now this ſhews that the Matter contained in theſe Bubbles, which at firſt is quite tranſparent, being a very rare and homogeneous Fluid, appears afterwards like Steam when it is mixed with the Air. But I thought I ſhould make a concluſive Experiment if I could obſerve the Effects of a very hot Steam conveyed under boiling Water. Therefore when an * Æolipile had boiled till all the Air was driven out of the Water it contained, without taking it off the Fire, I immerſed its Pipe into a Veſſel of Water which had juſt been boiled, and immediately the Steam that iſſued from the Pipe roſe up in very large Bubbles thro' the Water, and made it appear to boil violently. I then held a large Glaſs of cold Water, ſo that the Pipe of the boiling Æolipile was immerſed in it; at firſt none of theſe Bubbles appeared, for the Steam, being then condenſed by the cold Water, was mixed thro' it, making a very loud and uncommon Noiſe: but as ſoon as the Water in the Glaſs grew very hot, this Noiſe ceaſed, and the Steam, being no longer condenſed, roſe in large Bubbles, as before, and made the Water appear to boil with great Violence.

Theſe

---

* An *Æolipile* is a hollow Globe of Iron or Copper, into which is ſcrewed a long Pipe, whoſe End is commonly bent into a Curve; it has a very ſmall Orifice, out of which the Steam iſſues with great Violence, when Water is boiled in the *Æolipile*. See it delineated in Fig. 5.

These Obfervations and Experiments feem to difcover fully to us the Nature of thofe Bubbles that afcend thro' boiling Water ; and lead me to make fome further Remarks on the Degrees of Heat that different Liquors acquire in boiling.

The Parts of a Fluid neareſt the Bottom of a Veſſel grow hot firſt, and being then expanded and made lighter, they afcend and change Place with the colder and heavier Parts, which occaſions that inteſtine Motion we perceive in Liquors while they are growing hot. And thus the Heat of the Whole will continue to increaſe, until thoſe Particles, that are in contact with the Bottom of the Veſſel, acquire fuch a Degree of Heat as will give them a repelling Force fufficient to overcome the Weight of the Atmoſphere, the Weight of the incumbent Fluid, and the Tenacity of its Particles, and then they will be fuddenly expanded into Bubbles of Steam, and afcend quickly to the Top, without communicating this Heat to the furrounding Fluid. For as thefe Bubbles have a Degree of Heat but little fuperior to that of the Fluid, and juſt fufficient to keep them expanded, if they were to lofe any of it, by communicating it to the Fluid in their Afcent, they would all difappear before they got to the Surface, as the very fmall ones do which afcend but flowly ; or if

the

the whole Fluid was to grow at once as hot as
the Bubbles, it would, like them be all turned into
an elaftic Steam. And therefore the Fluid itfelf
cannot grow hotter than it was when thefe Bubbles began to afcend; but muft all boil away
in the fame Degree of Heat. [F] Provided
it be fuch a Fluid as will not grow denfer,
or more vifcid and tenacious by boiling, of
this kind are Mercury, Water, Spirit of Wine,
and feveral others, for thefe Fluids are found to
boil refpectively with 600, 212, and 175 Degrees
of Heat, and afterwards they do not grow hotter.
The Reafon of which is plain, for whilft the Preffure upon a Fluid, and its Denfity and Tenacity
continue the fame, the fame Degree of Heat will
always be fufficient to feparate its Particles and
expand them into Steam ; which is the greateft
Effect that Fire can produce on any Fluid without
actually inflaming it. Hence it is obvious that
an additional Preffure on boiling Liquors, or an
encreafe of their Denfity or Tenacity, will, by
keeping their Particles more ftrongly together, en-
able

[F] That thefe Bubbles are really hotter than the other
Parts of the Fluid I found by immerfing a Mercurial Thermometer with *Fahrenheit's* Scale into a Veffel of boiling Water, for it rofe one Degree higher when held among the Bubbles, where they were meft numerous, than it did in the other
Parts of the Water.

able them to bear a greater Degree of Heat before they are expanded into Steam and begin to boil. It is very obfervable that all oily Liquors, which refract the Rays of Light more ftrongly than others do, acquire alfo a much greater Heat in boiling. Thus Oil of Turpentine and other thin effential Oils, that are procured by Diftillation, boil with about 560 Degrees of Heat, which how-ever as the boiling continues is always encreafing ; the more volatile Parts flying away, and leaving the Refidue thicker, more vifcid, and fufceptible of greater Heat.

Common vegetable and animal Oils begin to boil with 600 Degrees of Heat, which is the fame with that of boiling Mercury, and therefore the greateft Heat that can be meafured by a Mercurial Thermometer. But it has been found, by the Expanfion of an Iron Rod, that Oils grow conti-nually hotter by boiling, and at length their Heat encreafes fo much that they burft into Flame.

There is indeed one Obfervation, which, if true, would contradict what I have faid as to the Heat of boiling Liquors being in fome Meafure owing to their Vifcidity ; for it is commonly faid that Tar, which is a vifcid Liquor, boils with fo fmall a Degree of Heat, that the Workmen fkim the Drofs off it with their Hands. But this I found to be only the Appearance of boiling, for

M   having

having placed a Veffel of Tar on the Fire; as foon as the Thermometer fhewed it to be a little hotter than the human Blood, a great Quantity of Air rofe out of it in Froth and Bubbles, carrying up fome Drofs with it, and then I could eafily bear to hold my Finger in it; but foon after when the Tar began really to boil the Thermometer rofe as high as it does in boiling Water, and was ftill rifing. For Tar, when one half of it is boiled away, becomes Pitch; and it is well known that boiling Pitch is hotter than boiling Water; fo that this Experiment correfponds exactly with the Theory I have laid down in regard to the Heat of boiling Liquors.

Hitherto we have confidered only the Effects of fuch Degrees of Heat as are great enough to expand Liquors into large Bubbles and make them boil, or to raife a vifible Steam from their Surface. But I find it neceffary (for a Reafon I fhall mention prefently) to confider alfo the Effects of the leffer Degrees of Heat, down to that which is juft fufficient to keep Liquors in a ftate of Fluidity.

It is generally allowed that Heat keeps Bodies fluid, by caufing their Particles in fome Meafure to repel each other, and thereby preventing them from coming into fuch clofe Contact as would render

render them hard. Now I fhall fhew from Experiments that all Degrees of Heat above what is neceffary to keep Liquors fluid, will raife from their Surface (provided they are not vifcid) fome kind of Steam, which, for Diftinction's fake, I fhall call an *Effluvium*. Under a large Glafs fet a Cup of Water, not hot enough to emit any vifible Steam, and let the Glafs be expofed to the cold Air, a Dew will foon appear on its Infide. Here an Effluvium is raifed from the Water, but it rifes too flowly and in too fmall a Quantity to become vifible till it is condenfed on the Glafs. As Steam rifes from hot Liquors more abundantly when the Preffure of the Atmofphere is taken away, it may be fuppofed that this Effluvium will alfo rife more copioufly from colder Liquors in the fame Cafe, as we fhall fee it really does by what follows. From a great Number of Experiments made with Spirits of Wine, of different Degrees of Strength, I found that, at a Medium, the Quantities loft in the fame time in a clofe Receiver full of Air, in one only half full of Air, in Air rarefied two and forty times, and in the open Air, were nearly in the Proportion of 1, $1\frac{5}{7}$, 6, and 48. The fame kind of Spirit was ufed in each Experiment, the Time was 24 Hours, and the Spirits were contained in equal Cups, fo that their Quantities and Surfaces were as nearly equal as might be. That all the Spirit ufed in each Experiment might be in the fame Circumftances, before I put it into

the

the Cups I drew from it all the Air I could by the Air-pump, which could not rarefy the Air in the Receiver more than two and forty times, it was neceffary to do this, becaufe the Spirit loft five or fix Grains in a few Minutes while the Air was drawing from it by the firft Exhauftion of the Receiver, and a Quantity lefs and lefs during the fecond and third Exhauftions. A Cup of Water when in a warm Room loft one Grain on the firft Exhauftion, and when it had afterwards ftood in the exhaufted Receiver for 24 Hours it loft two Grains and a Half, while the fame Quantity of Water loft 35 Grains in the open Air; but Ice that was thawing, or Water with Ice in it, did not lofe any thing in the exhaufted Receiver, or in a clofe Receiver full of Air. Thefe Experiments were made in a large Room without a Fire, and the Fluids were of the fame Temperature, whofe loffes I compared together.

The Spirit of Wine, which is fo eafily rarefied by Heat, and which (as it never freezes) has always more Heat than is fufficient to keep it fluid, loft in every Experiment confiderably more than Water did in the fame Circumftances; and as Water did not lofe any of its Weight, when it had not more Heat than was neceffary to keep it fluid, I think the rifing of an Effluvium from thefe Liquors may juftly be afcribed to the repelling Force given to their Particles by certain Degrees of Heat. The

Air

Air in the Receiver did not contribute to this Effect, but on the Contrary prevented it, in a great Measure, by its Pressure, for the more Air was drawn from the Receiver, the greater Quantity of this Effluvium arose. I observed, that when the Air was rarefied two and forty times, the Effluvium that rose from the Spirit, which was sometimes near forty Grains in twenty-four Hours, not being supported by a sufficient Quantity of Air, and losing its first Elasticity by being very much expanded, fell by its Weight to the Bottom, and covered it and the lower Parts of the Receiver with Moisture. But none, or very little, of this Moisture appeared when only one half of the Air was drawn out of the Receiver, for the Effluvium which then ascended, (amounting generally to eight or nine Grains) was supported by the remaining Air; but when I rarefied this Air suddenly, as in an Experiment before mentioned, (Page 59.) the Effluvium was immediately gathered into a vast Number of visible Drops, and fell to the Bottom. This plainly shews that the Effluvia which are raised from Liquors, by these very small Degrees of Heat, cannot continue suspended, unless they are supported by a sufficient Quantity of Air.

I thought it necessary to make these Experiments and Observations, in order to obviate an Objection which might be made to the Principle I
have

have endeavoured to eftablifh. For as it is found that Fluids lofe of their Weight both in an ex-haufted Receiver, and in the open Air, it might be faid that this lofs proceeded from the fame Caufe in both Cafes, and therefore that common Evaporation did not depend on the diffolving Power of the Air. But from thefe Experiments, I think, we might give a fufficient Anfwer to fuch an Ob-jection. For it appears firft; that Ice, or Water that has no more Heat than is neceffary to keep it fluid, lofe nothing of their Weight in an ex-haufted Receiver, tho' they lofe very confiderably in the open Air. Secondly; The Quantity which the Spirit of Wine loft by Evaporation in the open Air was eight times greater than what it loft in the fame time by an Effluvium, when the Air in the Receiver was rarefied two and forty times; therefore the Caufe of Evaporation muft be a much more powerful one than that which raifed the Effluvium. And further, the Quantity loft by Evaporation was forty-eight times greater than what was loft, in the fame time, by an Ef-fluvium when the Receiver was full of Air; there-fore, fuppofing the fame Effluvium to rife from it in the open Air, we muft allow that of the whole Quan-tity which the Spirit of Wine loft in the open Air, one Part only in forty-eight could be owing to that Effluvium which is occafioned merely by its Heat, confequently forty-feven Parts muft have been carried off by fome very powerful Action of the

Air;

Air; which muſt alſo be the ſole Cauſe of the Evaporation of Ice or very cold Water, which are found not to emit any Effluvia in an exhauſted Receiver. And this Action of the Air I have ſhewn to be its diſſolving Power.

Before we conclude, it may not be amiſs to take a general View of the important Purpoſes which Air is contrived to anſwer, and of the Means by which it is adapted to theſe ſeveral Purpoſes. By its Subtilty and Elaſticity it is capable of being eaſily taken into the Lungs of Animals; and by its attracting and diſſolving Power it carries on that Perſpiration, both internal and external, which we find is neceſſary to the Preſervation of Life. By the ſame Power it takes away the ſuper-fluous Moiſture from Trees and Plants, and there-by promotes Vegetation. By the ſame Power it raiſes and ſuſtains aqueous Vapours, and its Tem-perature and Denſity being eaſily changed, it re-turns them again in Rain and Dew, and thus keeps up a continual Circulation of Moiſture. By the ſame Power it contributes to the Support of Fire, by carrying off from burning Bodies all ſuch Fumes and Vapours as would otherwiſe extinguiſh them.

By its Weight and Preſſure on the Surface of Fluids it keeps their Particles together and enables them to bear (without being diſperſed

in

in Steam) fuch Degrees of Heat as are neceffary for all thofe Ufes to which boiling Liquors are applied. By the fame Preffure it raifes Water in Pumps and other Hydraulick Engines.

And laftly; we may add to thefe, all the various Purpofes to which the Winds are fubfervient; and which are too many to be enumerated, and too well known to require being particularly mentioned.

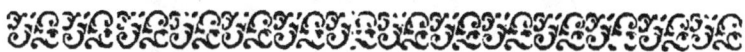

Obſervations *and* Conjectures

On the Nature of the

AURORA BOREALIS

AND THE

TAILS of COMETS.

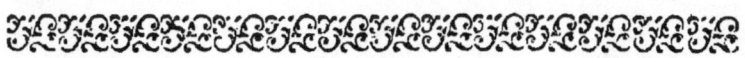

OBSERVATIONS

AND

CONJECTURES, &c.

HAVING obferved that fome late Writers, who endeavour to revive the exploded Hypothefis of an univerfal *Plenum*, bring Arguments in favour of their Opinion from what Sir *Ifaac Newton* fays of the Afcent of Comets' Tails in a Direction oppofite to the Sun; I was induced to reconfider his Account of that Matter, which, I own, never appeared fatis-

factory

factory to me; tho' I agree intirely with him that this Phænomenon affords a sufficient Proof of a *Vacuum* in the Celestial Regions. As this is a Subject of some Importance in Physicks I shall, in the following Essay, first, mention such Objections as occur to me against Sir *Isaac*'s Opinion as to the Cause of the Ascent of Comets' Tails; and then offer some Conjectures that may possibly lead to a further Knowledge of this Subject, leaving them to be confirmed or overthrown as future Observations and Experiments shall determine. For I think that Conjectures, or Hypotheses, when rendered probable by some Experiments, and proposed with Caution, may be of great Use by directing our Enquiries into some certain Channel.

That I may proceed methodically, I shall begin by relating the Phænomena of Comets as observed by *Newton*, and other accurate Astronomers, for I shall have Occasion to refer frequently to them.

It appears that a Comet is a kind of Planet which revolves round the Sun in a very excentric Orbit, and recedes much farther from the Sun in its *Aphelion* than any of the Planets; it is not visible until it comes down into the Planetary Regions, and then appears surrounded with a dense Atmosphere,

Atmosphere, and from the Side opposite to the
Sun it emits a shining Train which we call its Tail;
this near the Comet is of the same Thickness or Diameter with the Body, but grows somewhat
thicker towards the other End. It is at its first
Appearance very short, and encreases as the Comet approaches towards the Sun, and immediately after its *Perihelion* the Tail is longest and most
luminous, and then is generally observed to be
somewhat bent, and to be Convex towards those
Parts to which the Comet moves; the Convex
Side being rather brighter and better defined than
the Concave Side. When the Tail arrives at its
greatest Length which in some Comets has been
computed to be 60 or 70 Millions of Miles, it
quickly decreases and soon vanishes entirely, about
the same time that the Comet itself ceases to be
seen. The Matter of which the Tail is formed
is exceedingly rare, and so very pellucid that the
Light of the smallest Stars suffers no Diminution
in passing thro' it, for Sir *Isaac Newton* observes:
' The extraordinary Rarity of Comets' Tails may
' be collected from the Stars shining thro' them,
' for the smallest Stars are observed to shine with-
' out any loss of Splendor thro' the Tails which
' are of an immense Thickness, and are also il-
' luminated by the Light of the Sun.'*

Thefe

* Caudarum infignis raritas colligitur ex Aftris per eas
Tranflucentibus. — Per Immenfam vero Caudarum Craffitudi-

Thefe are the principal Phænomena of Comets, and it is from hence we muft deduce whatever we can know of the Subftance of which the Tails confift, or of the Reafon why they are always thrown off from the Head of the Comet, in a Direction nearly oppofite to the Sun. And with thefe Phænomena I propofe to compare the Opinions which are commonly received concerning this Matter. Sir *Ifaac* tells us, there were three different Opinions about Comets' Tails; *viz.* that they were only Rays of the Sun propagated thro' the tranfparent Head of the Comet. Or that they arofe from the Refraction of the Light in its Paffage from the Head of the Comet to the Earth. Or, laftly, that they confifted of Clouds and Vapours continually rifing from the Head of the Comet, and going off in a Direction oppofite to the Sun. The firft and fecond of thefe Opinions he refutes, and adopts the third, and proves by feveral Arguments, that the Tail muft confift of fome kind of Vapour arifing continually from the Head of the Comet. The Caufe of its afcending always from the Sun he affigns in another Paragraph, which I

shall

---

nem, Lnce pariter Solis illuftratam, Aftra minima abfque Claritatis Detrimento tranflucere nofcuntur. *Principia,* Page 515. Edit. 2da.

fhall now quote at length, tranflating it as faith-
fully as I can; it is as follows:

‘ The Afcent of Tails from the Atmofphere
‘ of Comets and their Progrefs towards the Parts
‘ oppofite to the Sun, *Kepler* afcribes to the Action
‘ of the Rays of Light, carrying with them the
‘ Matter of which the Tails confift. And that fo
‘ very thin an Air or Vapour fhould yield to the
‘ Action of the Rays, in Spaces void of refiftance,
‘ is not altogether againft Reafon ; altho’ in our
‘ Regions, clogged with refifting Matter, the folar
‘ Rays cannot fenfibly impel denfe Bodies. Others
‘ think that there may be fome Particles of Mat-
‘ ter in their own Nature light, as well as fome
‘ that are heavy, and that the Matter of the Tails
‘ is of the former Sort, and by its Levity afcends
‘ from the Sun. But fince the Gravity of all ter-
‘ reftial Bodies is proportional to their quantity of
‘ Matter, and cannot in the fame Body be in-
‘ creafed or diminifhed, I fufpect that this Afcent
‘ of the Tails arifes rather from the Rarefaction
‘ of their Matter. Smoke afcends in a Chimney
‘ by the Impulfe of the Air in which it floats ;
‘ that Air, being rarefied by Heat, and its fpeci-
‘ fic Gravity thereby diminifhed, afcends and
‘ carries the Smoke with it. Why then fhould
‘ not the Tail of a Comet afcend in the fame Man-
‘ ner from the Sun? for the folar Rays do not
‘   e any Medium thro’ which they pafs, but
‘ in

‘ in Reflection or Refraction, the reflecting Parti-
‘ cles by that Action grow warm, and heat the
‘ ætherial Air (*auram Ætheream*) with which they
‘ are mixed, which being rarefied by this Heat,
‘ and the fpecific Gravity by which it tended to
‘ the Sun being thereby diminifhed, it will afcend
‘ and carry with it the reflecting Particles of which
‘ the Tail is formed : it conduces alfo to the
‘ Afcent of thefe Vapours that they revolve round
‘ the Sun, and therefore endeavour to recede from
‘ it ; while the Atmofphere of the Sun either is
‘ at reft, or revolves more flowly with fuch Mo-
‘ tion as it can acquire from the Rotation of the
‘ Sun round its Axis. Thefe are the Caufes of
‘ the Afcent of the Tails in the Neighbourhood
‘ of the Sun, where the Orbit has a greater Cur-
‘ vature, and the Comet moves in a denfer, and
‘ therefore heavier Atmofphere of the Sun, and
‘ then emits a Tail of a greater Length. For the
‘ Tails which then arife by preferving their own
‘ Motion, and at the fame time gravitating to-
‘ wards the Sun, will revolve about the Sun in
‘ *Ellipfes* juft as their Heads do ; and by that Mo-
‘ tion will always accompany their Heads and ad-
‘ here to them moft freely. For the Gravity of
‘ thofe Vapours towards the Sun will no more caufe
‘ the Tails to fall from the Heads to the Sun, than
‘ it will caufe the Heads to fall from the Tails, but
‘ they muft both, by their common Gravity, fall
‘ together to the Sun, or both together be retarded
‘ in their Afcent from it : and confequently their

‘ Gravity

' Gravity will not hinder the Heads and Tails of
' Comets eafily to receive (from the above-men-
' tioned or other Caufes) any Pofition whatever
' in refpeet to each other, or to keep this Pofition
' afterwards moft freely.'§

We find in this Account that Sir *Ifaac* afcribes
the Afcent of Comets' Tails to their being rarer
and lighter, and moving round the Sun more
fwiftly, than the folar Atmofphere with which he
fuppofes them to be furrounded, whilft in the
Neighbourhood of the Sun; he fays alfo that
whatever Pofition (in refpect to each other) the
Head and Tail of a Comet then receive, they will
keep the fame afterwards moft freely, and in another Place he obferves, ' that the celeftial Spaces
' muft be entirely void of any Power of refifting,
' fince not only the folid Bodies of the Planets
' and Comets, but even the exceeding thin Va-
' pours, of which Comets' Tails are formed, move
' thro' thofe Spaces with immenfe Velocity, and yet
' with the greateft Freedom.'‖ — I cannot help
thinking that this Account is liable to many Diffi-
culties and Objections, and that it feems not very
confiftent with itfelf or with the Phænomena.

O   I do

§ *Principia,* Page 514.   ‖ Ibid.

I do not know that we have any Proof of the Exiftence of a folar Atmofphere of any confiderable Extent, nor are we any where taught how to guefs at the Limits of it. It is evident that the Exiftence of fuch an Atmofphere cannot be proved merely by the Afcent of Comets' Tails from the Sun, as that Phænomenon may poffibly arife from fome other Caufe. However let us fuppofe, for the prefent, that the Afcent of Comets' Tails is owing to an Atmofphere furrounding the Sun, and fee how the Effects arifing from thence will agree with the Phænomena. When a Comet comes into the folar Atmofphere, and is then defcending almoft directly to the Sun, if the Vapours which compofe the Tail are raifed up from it by the fuperior Denfity and Weight of that Atmofphere, they muft rife into thofe Parts that the Comet has left, and therefore at that time they may appear in a Direction oppofite to the Sun. But as foon as the Comet comes near the Sun, and moves in a Direction nearly at right Angles with the Direction of its Tail, the Vapours which then arife, partaking of the great Velocity of the Comet, and being fpecifically lighter than the *Medium* in which they move, and being vaftly expanded thro' it, muft neceffarily fuffer a Refiftance immenfely greater than what the fmall and denfe Body of the Comet meets with, and confequently cannot poffibly

fibly keep up with it, but muſt be driven back-
wards by the Reſiſtance of that Medium into a
Line directed towards the Parts which the Comet
has left, and therefore can no longer appear in a
Direction oppoſite to the Sun. And in like Manner when a Comet paſſes its *Perihelion*, and begins
to aſcend from the Sun, it certainly ought to appear ever after with its Tail behind it, or in a
Direction pointed towards the Sun ; for if the
Tail of the Comet be ſpecifically lighter than the
Medium in which it moves with ſo great Velocity,
it muſt be juſt as impoſſible it ſhould move foremoſt, as it is that a Torch moved ſwiftly thro'
the Air ſhould project its Flame and Smoke before it. Since therefore we find that the Tail of a
Comet, even when it is aſcending from the Sun,
moves foremoſt and appears in a Direction nearly
oppoſite to the Sun, I think we muſt conclude that
the Comet and its Tail do not move in a Medium
heavier and denſer than the Matter of which the
Tail conſiſts, and conſequently that the conſtant
Aſcent of the Tail from the Sun muſt be owing to
ſome other Cauſe. For that the ſolar Atmoſphere
ſhould have Denſity and Weight ſufficient to raiſe
up the Vapours of a Comet from the Sun, and yet
not be able to give any ſenſible Reſiſtance to theſe
Vapours in their rapid Progreſs thro' it, are two
things inconſiſtent with each other. And therefore,
ſince the Tail of a Comet is found to move as
freely as the Body does, we ought rather to con-

O 2

clude that the celeſtial Spaces are void of all reſiſting Matter, than that they are filled with a
ſolar Atmoſphere, be it ever ſo rare.

But there is, I think, a further Conſideration
which will ſhew that the received Opinion, as
to the Aſcent of Comets' Tails, is not agreeable to the Phænomena, and may at the ſame
time ſerve to lead us to ſome Knowledge of the
Matter of which theſe Tails conſiſt ; which I ſuſ-
pect is of a very different Nature from what it has
been hitherto ſuppoſed to be. Sir *Iſaac* ſays, the
Vapours, of which the Tail of a Comet conſiſts,
grow hot by reflecting the Rays of the Sun, and
thereby warm and rarefy the Medium which ſur-
rounds them ; which muſt therefore aſcend from
the Sun, and carry with it the reflecting Particles
of which the Tail is formed ; for he always ſpeaks
of the Tail as ſhining by reflected Light. But one
would rather imagine, from the Phænomena, that
the Matter which forms a Comet's Tail has not
the leaſt ſenſible Power of reflecting the Rays of
Light. And this I think appears from Sir *Iſaac*'s
Obſervation which I have quoted already ; for he
affirms, that the Light of the ſmalleſt Stars, coming to us through the immenſe thickneſs of a Comet's Tail, does not ſuffer the leaſt Diminution. ~~But farther~~, And yet if the Tail can reflect the
Light of the Sun ſo copiouſly, as it muſt do
if

if its great Splendor be derived from thence, it
muft undoubtedly have the fame Effect on the
Light of the Stars ; that is, it muft reflect back
the Light, which comes from the Stars behind
it, and by fo doing muft intercept them from
our Sight, confidering its vaft thicknefs, and how
exceedingly flender a Ray is that comes from
a fmall Star, or if it did not intercept their whole
Light, it muft, at leaft, increafe their twinkling. But we do not find that it has even
this fmall Effect, for thofe Stars that appear
thro' the Tail are not obferved to twinkle
more than others in their Neighbourhood. Since
therefore this Fact is fupported by Obfervations,
what can be a plainer Proof that the Matter of a
Comet's Tail has no Power of reflecting the Rays
of Light? and confequently that it muft be a felf-
fhining Subftance. But the fame thing will further
appear from confidering that Bodies reflect and refract Light by one and the fame Power ; and therefore if Comets' Tails want the Power of refracting
the Rays of Light, they muft alfo want the Power
of reflecting them. Now, that they want this refracting Power appears from hence, if that great
Column of tranfparent Matter which forms a Comet's Tail, and moves either in a *Vacuum*, or in
fome Medium of a different Denfity from its own,
had any Power of refracting a Ray of Light, coming thro' it from a Star to us, that Ray muft be
turned far out of its way in paffing over the great
Diftance

Diftance between the Comet and the Earth ; and, therefore, we fhould very fenfibly perceive the fmalleft Refraction that the Light of the Stars might fuffer in paffing thro' a Comet's Tail. The Confequence of fuch a Refraction muft be very remarkable, the Stars that lie near the Tail would appear double, for they would appear in their proper Places by their direct Rays, and we fhould fee their Images behind the Tail, by means of their Rays which it might refract to our Eyes; and thofe Stars that were really behind the Tail would difappear, their Rays being turned afide from us by Refraction. In fhort, it is eafy to imagine what ftrange Alterations would be made in the apparent Places of the fixed Stars by the Tails of Comets, if they had a Power of refract- ing their Light; which could not fail to be taken Notice of, if any fuch ever happened. But fince Aftronomers have not mentioned any fuch apparent Changes of Place among the Stars, I take it for granted that the Stars feen thro' all Parts of a Comet's Tail appear in their proper Places, and with their ufual Colours, and confequently I infer that the Rays of Light fuffer no Refraction in paffing thro' a Comet's Tail. And thence I con- clude (as before) that the Matter of a Comet's Tail has not the Power of refracting or reflecting the Rays of Light, and muft therefore be a lucid or felf-fhining Subftance.

And

And thus if I have argued rightly from the Phænomena, it muſt appear, that the Tail of a Comet does not conſiſt of aqueous or other Vapours, that ſhine by reflecting the Light of the Sun, but is a very rare, tranſparent and lucid Subſtance, which has no ſort of Effect on the Rays of Light that paſs thro' it, and that it is thrown off from the dark Hemiſphere of the Comet in a Direction oppoſite to the Sun, not by the ſuperior Weight and Denſity of any circumambient Medium, but by ſome other Cauſe that has not yet been diſcovered.

This ſeems to me to be all the Knowledge we can acquire of the Nature and Properties of that Matter which form the Tails of Comets, by attending merely to the Phænomenon itſelf. But perhaps we may be able to extend this Knowledge ſomewhat further, if we could find any other Phænomenon in Nature which reſembles this of Comets' Tails, and can become acquainted with any kind of Matter that has the ſame Properties with that of which they are formed. Now I have often obſerved a Phænomenon that, I think, very ſtrongly reſembles the Tail of a Comet, both in its Appearance, and in the Nature of its Subſtance. We frequently ſee a very rare, tranſparent, and lucid Subſtance thrown off, in a Direction nearly oppoſite

to

to the Sun, from the dark Hemiſphere of the Earth, and principally from the more Northern and colder Regions of our Atmoſphere. This Appearance is ſo luminous that it has been from thence called the *Aurora Borealis*; it is now ſo common and well known that I ſhall not deſcribe it particularly, and will only take Notice of thoſe Circumſtances in which it chiefly reſembles a Comet's Tail. Thoſe Northern Lights never appear, at leaſt in any remarkable Degree, ſoon after Sunſet or before Sun-riſe, tho' it may be then dark enough to make them viſible, but generally from about ten o'Clock at Night till one in the Morning; and the very long Streams of Light, which iſſue frequently from the Northern Parts of our Atmoſphere, ſeem ſtill to tend towards the Zenith of that Place where the Spectator is, and ſome times get beyond the Zenith, and appear to the Southward of it; which ſhews that theſe Streams of Light tend towards the Vertex of the Earth's Shadow, that is, towards the Part of the Heavens which is oppoſite to the Sun. From the great Length of theſe Streams of Light, which ſeem always moving upwards, we may conclude that they extend to a great Height in the Atmoſphere, and probably riſe far above it. For by the Accounts we have of an *Aurora Borealis*, obſerved in *England* on the Sixth of *March*, 1716, it was viſible from the Weſt Side of *Ireland*, to the Confines of *Ruſſia* and *Poland*, and probably farther to the Eaſt; ſo

that

that it extended at leaſt over thirty Degrees of Longitude, and from about the fiftieth Degree of Latitude over almoſt all the North of *Europe*, and at all Places it exhibited the ſame Appearances, nearly at the ſame time.‡

Now this great Body of luminous Matter which appears in an *Aurora Borealis*, being ſo very extenſive and ſometimes ſo very bright, muſt be viſible to a Spectator placed at a conſiderable Diſtance from the Earth, and ſhaded from the Sun's Light; and ſuch a Spectator would then ſee the Earth attended by a Train of Light in the Form of a Tail. It would probably appear ſmall in Proportion to the Earth's Diameter, it would ſeem unſteady, changeable in its Shape, and of a ſhort Continuance; but whilſt it laſted it muſt, both in its Direction, and in the Nature and Appearance of its Light, very much reſemble the Tail of a Comet. And if ſuch a Spectator was to obſerve the Earth for a Year he might perceive a further Reſemblance in this Reſpect between the Earth and a Comet; for as the Tail of a Comet appears only a ſhort time before and after its *Peribelion*, ſo he would ſee this luminous Matter riſe from the Earth frequently whilſt it was moving from the Autumnal to the Vernal Equinox, thro' the half of its Orbit that is neareſt to the

P   Sun,

‡ Philoſ. Tranſ. No. 347.

Sun, and very feldom during the other Part of
the Year, for we rarely fee an *Aurora Borealis* in the
Summer Months. Thus we find that the Matter
of an *Aurora Borealis* and that of a Comet's Tail
are very like each other in their Appearance, and
in their Situation, with refpect to the Sun and the
Bodies from which they flow. And if we examine
further, we fhall find that they have exactly the
fame Properties ; for the Matter of which the *Aurora Borealis* confifts is not only very rare, tranfparent and lucid, but is alfo found to have no fort
of Effect on the Rays of Light which pafs thro'
it. This I have often obferved, and particularly at
one time when there appeared here an *Aurora Borealis*,† which for its Extent, for the Quantity,
Brightnefs and Steadinefs of its Lights, was the
moft remarkable one I ever faw ; fome Part of it
appeared like very denfe white Clouds, illuminated
by a full Moon, but with a more vivid Brightnefs ;
and yet thro' one of the denfeft and whiteft of thefe
Clouds, I could plainly fee the fmalleft Star in
the *Pliades*, and could not perceive that its Splen-
dour was at all diminifhed, or that it even twink-
led more than it did before this lucid Matter was
interpofed, which, as it moved with a quick tre-
mulous Motion, muft have at leaft increafed the
twinkling of the Stars, if it had any fort of Effect
on the Rays which paffed thro' it. Since then the
Matter of a Comet's Tail, and that of the *Aurora
Borealis*

† *October* 16th or 17th, 1763.

Borealis are alike in their Appearance, and agree alfo in their Properties, we have fome Reafon to fuppofe that they are Subftances of the fame Kind.

Having gained this Step, we may go on in our Enquiries, and try if any other Subftance, that we are better acquainted with, has the fame Properties with the Subftance of which Comets' Tails and the *Aurora Borealis* are formed. It is now well known that our Atmofphere abounds with electric Matter, which is more or lefs contained in all Bodies ; this Matter is never vifible but whilft it is paffing from one Body to another, thro' the Air or a Vacuum, it then appears to be a very rare, fubtle, fhining Subftance. We often fee it flafhing from one Cloud to another, or into the Earth, with great Velocity and Brightnefs, and then we give it the Name of Lightning ; and in the fame Manner when we bring our Finger near a Bar of Iron ftrongly electrified, we fee very bright Sparks iffue from it to our Finger. It feems that Air, in its common State of Condenfation, refifts the Egrefs of the electric Matter from Bodies in which it is accumulated, efpecially if they are round and fmooth, and when it forces its Way it feems to come out, as it were, all at once, and in a very condenfed State, and therefore it appears very bright. But if the Air be confiderably rarefied its Refiftance is thereby greatly leffened, and

P 2   the

the electric Matter cannot be accumulated in a Body furrounded by fuch Air, for in that Cafe, as faft as it is communicated to the Body it will iffue out from various Parts of it in fmall Streams of a faint Light, as will appear from fome Experiments I fhall have Occafion to mention prefently.

Now fince a folid Body and a Cloud, when electrified in denfe Air, will both difcharge their Fire in the fame Manner, that is, fuddenly and in bright Sparks, or large bright Flafhes, we muft conclude, from Analogy, that when they are both electrified in Air much rarefied, they will then likewife difcharge their Fire in the fame Manner, and confequently that an electrified Cloud, raifed into the higher and rarer Parts of the Atmofphere, will difcharge its Fire in continued Streams of faint Light. And as we fometimes fee faint flafhes of Lightning in a Summer Evening after Sun-fet, tho' no Clouds appear; fo if the Vapours which rife into the higher Part of the Atmofphere, tho' not formed into Clouds, carry up with them the electric Matter, they muft difcharge it in continued Streams of faint Light, juft as a Cloud would do; and thofe Streams of Light in the higher Parts of the Atmofphere muft exactly reprefent to us the Appearance of an *Aurora Borealis*. Any one will readily perceive a ftrong Refemblance between the *Aurora*

rora Borealis and the electric Fire discharged from
a Body in rarefied Air, who will make the following Experiments.

Let the Air be almoft exhaufted out of a Glafs
Globe or Cylinder, and let it be turned by a Machine and rubbed as ufual; the electric Fire will
then appear in the Infide of the Globe, fhooting
out in various Branches of faint Light, croffing
each other in all Directions, and this Light will
fometimes appear tinged with different Colours;
when the Air is very much rarefied the Light
appears white, and grows more of a purple Colour as more Air is admitted into the Globe. I
found this Experiment fucceed beft when I held
in my Hand the Cufhion with which the Globe
was rubbed, and preffed it fometimes clofely and
fometimes flightly to the Globe. I made alfo
another Experiment to the fame Purpofe. A Cylinder 20 Inches high, and about 5 in diameter,
having a pretty thick Brafs Wire put thro' the
Top, was almoft exhaufted, then being myfelf
electrified, I moved my Finger towards the Top
of the Wire, and immediately I faw every Spark
that came from my Finger divided into a Mul-
titude of fmall Streams of Light iffuing from the
Wire at right Angles to it, and in different Directions. When I took hold of the Wire I could
fee but little Light in the Cylinder, fo found it

was neceſſary to keep my Finger at a ſmall Diſ-tance, and let the electric Matter come to the Wire in ſucceſſive Sparks. I thought the Lights that iſſued from the Wire were brighteſt when it was oyled, and when the Air was about 30 times rarer than the outward Air. Several Perſons al-moſt as ſoon as they ſaw the electric Lights com-pared them to the Appearance of the *Aurora Bo-realis* ; and certainly theſe two Phænomena reſemble each other entirely. both in the Colours of their Light, and in the Quickneſs of their Motions. For when the Air in the Glaſs-Globe was very much rarefied, the electric Lights appeared very white, and became more of a purple Colour as more Air was admitted into the Globe ; juſt ſo the long Streams of Light in the *Aurora Borealis* are very white on their upper Parts where the Air about them is much rarefied, and are often of a purple Colour on their lower Parts which are in denſer Air. And as in the Globe the electric Lights appear in greater Abundance when the Air has a particular Degree of Denſity than in other Caſes ; ſo the quick Appearing and Diſap-pearing of the Streams of Light in the *Aurora Borealis* may poſſibly ariſe from a Charge of Den-ſity in the higher Parts of the Atmoſphere. For, where the Air is ſo very thin it may be ſubject to very ſudden Condenſations, Rarefactions occa-ſioned by the Motion of the Winds, and I have

observed

obferved thofe Lights to be more unfteady in a windy Night than when it was calm.

But the electric Matter appears to be of the fame kind of Subftance which forms the *Aurora Borealis,* and the Tails of Comets, by its having alfo that remarkable Property of letting the Rays of Light pafs thro' it, without having any fort of Effect upon them. And this I found by feveral Experiments; for I obferved that fmall Rays of Light, paffing over fharp Points, and by the Edges of Knives, from whence the electric Matter iffued abundantly, were affected in the very fame Manner as when thefe Points and Edges were not electrified. Having provided a large Pane of Glafs properly coated on both Sides with thin fheet Lead, I made two fmall Holes in the Lead, oppofite to each other, for a Ray of Light to pafs thro'; and I found this Ray was no more refracted in its Paffage thro' the Holes, when one Side of the Glafs was electrified *Plus,* and the other *Minus,* than it was before the Glafs was electrified at all, or after the electric Matter was difcharged, which fhews that the Accumulation, or the Abfence of this Matter no way contributed to encreafe or diminifh the refractive Power of the Glafs. I found that when Water was electrified no change was made either in its Power of refracting or reflecting the Rays of Light.

I made

I made many other Experiments of the same kind, too tedious to describe, and they all led me to conclude that the electric Matter had no sort of Effect on the Rays of Light that passed thro' it. Since then the electric Matter seems to be of the same Nature with that which forms the *Aurora Borealis*, and abounds much in the Atmosphere, and, when it gets into the rarer Parts of it, will, by its known Properties, exhibit to us an Appearance like that of the *Aurora Borealis*, we must acknowledge it to be a Cause really existing, and sufficient to explain this Phænomenon, and therefore we may ascribe the Appearance of an *Aurora Borealis* to the Rising of the electric Matter into the upper Regions of the Atmosphere. The following Observation will serve further to confirm this Opinion. In our Summer Months, when the electric Matter is frequently discharged from the lower Clouds in Lightning, and so returns to the Earth, we scarce ever see an *Aurora Borealis*; but at other times, when it is not usually discharged in Lightning, it may rise higher into the Atmosphere, and will occasion more frequent Appearances of this kind. And this probably is the Reason why these Appearances are more frequent in cold than in warm Climates, the former being less subject to Storms of Thunder and Lightning than the latter. In Countries that lie

far

far to the North the *Aurora Borealis* is faid to fhine much brighter than with us, and to appear almoft every Night.

As the preceding Confiderations feem to make it probable that the Tails of Comets confift of the fame kind of Subftance which forms the *Aurora Borealis*, and that this is no other than the electric Matter; I fhall affume this as a Principle, and try if I can from thence Account, in fome Meafure, for the Phænomenon of Comets' Tails, and in doing this I fhall have an Opportunity of making fome Obfervations which may ferve to fhew a further Refemblance between thofe three Subftances that I have compared together. The Earth, and all Bodies near it, contain more or lefs of the electric Matter, and tho' it may be accumulated in fome Bodies, and diminifhed in others, we cannot be fure that any Body may be totally deprived of it, but on the Contrary have great Reafon to think it can neither be increafed nor diminifhed in any Body beyond a certain Degree; we muft therefore fuppofe that it is contained in all Bodies in our folar Syftem. Some Bodies fuch as Glafs, Amber and others, that are called *Electrics*, attract and retain this Matter more ftrongly than thofe do which are called *Non-Electrics*, for an electric Body will draw this Matter

Q   from

from one that is not electric against which it is rubbed, and it will alfo ftop the electric Matter in its Progrefs from one Body to another, and therefore an electric Body is called a *Non-conductor*, in Oppofition to other Bodies thro' which the electric Matter readily paffes. But we find that any Body even the moft Electric, if fufficiently heated, will become a *Conductor*, or will let the electric Matter pafs from it very eafily, and therefore we conclude that Heat difpofes all Bodies readily to part with the electric Matter they contain, and we have an Inftance in the *Tourmalin* Stone that fome Bodies will always throw off an electric Matter merely by being heated. Now when a Comet comes down towards the Sun, from Regions of extreme Cold, and begins to acquire fome Degree of Heat, it will, like other Bodies, be difpofed to part with the electric Matter, which it may poffibly contain in great Abundance, and this Matter, when thrown off, will exhibit to us the Appearance of a fhining Train, as it does in the *Aurora Borealis*; and as the Comet comes to its *Perihelion*, and the Heat increafes, this Matter will iffue more abundantly, and the Train or Tail will increafe in Length, till upon the Comets' receding from the Sun the Heat will decreafe, and this Matter being pretty much exhaufted, the Tail will be contracted in its

Dimenfions,

Dimenfions, and at length will be too far removed, and grow too faint to be obferved.

As a Comet is expofed to vaft extremes of Heat and Cold, Light and Darknefs, we may well fup-pofe it to be uninhabited, and if fo it is not ne-ceffary that it fhould turn round its Axis, but may always keep the fame Face towards the Sun, as the Moon keeps the fame Face towards the Earth, and indeed it muft do fo if its Figure be that of an oblong Spheroid. Now the electric Matter which rifes from the Earth goes off into the colder Regions of the Atmofphere, and in a Direction nearly oppofite to the Sun, and I believe we have no Inftance of what we call the *Aurora Borealis* appearing between the Tropicks. Why then fhould not this Matter take the fame Courfe in its Progrefs from the Head of the Comet, and fly off from its dark Hemifphere, where its At-mofphere is colder and clearer, and where the Va-pours are thin, and, rifing more gradually, will give it an Opportunity of rifing along with them ; whilft on the other Hemifphere, which is expofed to the Sun, the Vapours muft rife very thick, and form Clouds which may intercept the electric Matter in its Progrefs, and collecting it together may return it back to the Head of the Comet in Lightning as our Clouds in hot Countries return their electric Matter into the Earth. Befides as

we

we find that the electric Matter paffes off from a
Body where it is rough or pointed much more
readily than where it is round and fmooth, fo it
is poffible that the Hemifphere of the Comet,
which is turned from the Sun, may be fo formed
as to part with the electric Matter more readily
than the other, which is turned towards the Sun;
and in whatever Direction the electric Matter is
thrown off from any Body we find it continues to
move with immenfe Velocity, as I obferved in
the Streams of electric Matter which iffued from
the Wire in the exhaufted Receiver. I obferved
alfo that thefe Streams did not grow much thicker
as they advanced in their Courfe, either in the exhaufted Globe or cylindrical Receiver; nor did
they feem difpofed to expand themfelves into the
Space that furrounded them, but went ftraight
forward juft as a Ray of folar Light would do. And
thus the Matter which iffues from a Comet pro-
ceeds in the fame Direction in which it is thrown
off, and forms that large Column, which we call
the Tail; and we fee that the Matter of which
the Tail confifts has very little or no Difpofition
to expand itfelf into the furrounding Spaces; for
the Tail is not much broader towards the End
than near the Head of the Comet. This I think
is a moft extraordinary Property, both of the
electric Matter, and of that which forms a Comet's Tail, and which is a further Argument for
concluding

concluding them to be of the same Nature, for they both fly off from the Body, in which they are, with great Velocity, which seems to argue a repulsive and expansive Force, yet they proceed as the Rays of Light do without expanding themselves laterally into the Spaces thro' which they pass.

And this remarkable Property seems well worth attending to in all our Enquiries concerning the electric Matter. At present we are so little acquainted with the true Nature of it, and so ignorant of the Substance which forms the Body of the Comet, that is not to be expected, we should be able to say how it can furnish such a vast Quantity of this electric Matter, or to assign with Certainty the Reason why the Tail of a Comet is thrown off from its dark Hemisphere in a Direction opposite to the Sun, rather than in any other Direction. Future Experiments and Observations will either confirm these Conjectures of mine or suggest others more probable ; but now we can only argue by Analogy from the rising of the electric Matter thro' the colder Regions of our Atmosphere in the *Aurora Borealis,* that the same Effect will take Place in the Atmosphere of a Comet, and from the same Cause, whatever that may be.

Sir

Sir *Isaac Newton* obferves the Tail of the Comet which came to its *Perihelion* on the eighth of *December*, 1680, appeared about the Middle of *January* following to be bent into a Curve. Now as the Tail was convex towards thofe Parts to which the Comet moved, this bending might feem to arife from its meeting with fome refifting Matter; but this Curvature was much lefs than what would arife from a refifting Matter denfer than the Tail, and whofe fuperior Gravity would be able to raife it up from the Sun ; for he tells us that on the 5th of *January* when the Tail was 40 Degrees long, its Chord, or a Line drawn from the Head of the Comet to the Extremity of its Tail, made an Angle of only 8 Degrees with a great Circle paffing thro' the Sun and Comet. But that this Curvature was not owing to any refifting Matter appears from hence, that the Tail muft be bent into a Curve tho' it met with no Refiftance; for it could not be a right Line unlefs all its Particles were projected in the fame Direction, and with the fame Velocity, and unlefs the Comet moved uniformly in a right Line. But the Comet moves in a Curve, and each Part of the Tail is projected in a Direction oppofite to the Sun, and at the fame time partakes of the Motion of the Comet ; fo that the different Parts of the Tail muft move on in Lines which diverge from each other; and a Line drawn from the Head of a Comet to the

Extremity

Extremity of the Tail will be parallel to a Line drawn from the Sun to the Place where the Comet was, when that Part of the Tail began to afcend, as Sir *Ifaac* obferves; and fo all the Chords, or Lines drawn from the Head of the Comet to the intermediate Parts of the Tail, will be refpectively parallel to Lines drawn from the Sun to the Places where the Comet was when thefe Parts of the Tail began to afcend. And therefore fince thefe Chords of the Tail will be of different Lengths, and parallel to different Lines, they muft make different Angles, with a great Circle paffing thro' the Sun and Comet, and confequently a Line paffing thro' their Extremities will be a Curve.

It is obferved that the convex Side of the Tail which is turned from the Sun is better defined and fhines a little brighter than the concave Side. Sir *Ifaac* accounts for this by faying, that the Vapour on the convex Side is frefher (that is, has afcended later) than that on the concave Side, and yet I cannot fee how the Particles on the convex Side can be thought to have afcended later than thofe on the concave Side which may be nearer to the Head of the Comet. I think it rather looks as if the Tail, in its rapid Motion, met with fome flight Refiftance juft fufficient to caufe a fmall Condenfation in that Side of it which moves foremoft, and which would occa-

fion

fion it to appear a little brighter and better defined than the other Side; which flight Refiftance
may arife from that fubtle Æther which is fuppofed
to be difperfed thro' the celeftial Regions, or from
this very electric Matter difperfed in the fame
Manner, if it be different from the Æther. Here
I muft obferve that the convex Side of the Tail,
which is turned from the Sun, being brighter than
the other Side, affords an additional Argument in
favour of what I have afferted, that the Tail does
not fhine by reflecting the Sun's Light. And this
leads me to fay fomething of that luminous Quality which we obferve in the electric Matter, and
by which I fuppofe the Tails of Comets to
fhine.

The Writers on Electricity tell us that the electric Matter carries off from Bodies certain fubtile
Particles of a fulphurous inflammable Nature, which
it kindles as foon as they are difengaged from the
Body, and thence it fhines. And this Account
is proved from its inflaming other Bodies, fuch as
warm Spirits, and from that fulphurous Smell
which always attends the electric Matter, and
which, any one will perceive from his Hand, if
he receives the electric Sparks on it for fome time,
and the fame Smell is more ftrongly perceived in
Places that have been ftruck by Lightning. Now
thefe

thefe inflammable Vapours which often abound in the Air, being carried up by the electric Matter, and kindled in the higher Parts of the Atmofphere, will caufe it to fhine and appear to us in the *Aurora Borealis*.

But perhaps it may be faid, that, without having recourfe to the electric Matter, we might fuppofe the Comet, or a great Part of it, to confift of fome very combuftible Matter which may take fire by a fmall Degree of Heat, and blaze out in fuch Abundance as to occafion that luminous Appearance we call the Tail. And this Hypothefis may appear at firft Sight more natural and probable than the one I have fuggefted; yet I imagine it will not be found fo, if we examine it attentively. For if the Comet were to take fire and blaze out as burning Bodies do with us, the elafticity of the Flame might indeed raife it to fome Diftance from the Body of the Comet, but then it would rife equally on all Sides, or rather to a greater Height on the Side next the Sun, where the Heat is greateft. And a Flame of this kind could not be carried up in a Direction oppofite to the Sun, unlefs it were by the fuperior Denfity and Weight of fome furrounding Medium which gravitates towards the Sun; juft as we find the Flame of burning Bodies is raifed upwards by the Preffure of the furrounding Air. But I have

R   fhewn,

shewn, in the former Part of this Essay, that a Medium denser and heavier than the Tail must resist and retard its Motion much more than that of the Comet, and therefore could never permit the Tail to move foremost as it sometimes does, but must cause it always to fall behind, and consequently to appear as directed towards the Sun when the Comet has passed its *Peribelion*, and is retiring from the Sun. So that in order to account for the constant Ascent of this luminous Matter in a Direction opposite to the Sun, we must have recourse to some Medium that has no sensible Gravity, and that is apt to move in some particular Direction from the Body in which it is, and with such Velocity as to carry the burning Matter to a vast Distance from the Comet before it is entirely consumed. Now I believe we do not know of any Medium that has these Properties except that which we call the electric Matter. For it seems no more affected by the Force of Gravity than the Rays of Light are, and when it moves freely it is apt to go on in the Direction in which it sets out, as I observed before, and then it moves with such a Velocity as we cannot measure. For it has been found to pass thro' a Wire two Miles and a Half in Length, as it were, instantaneously, and probably its Velocity is not inferior to that of the Rays of Light. This Medium therefore seems not only capable of kindling
such

such subtile inflammable Particles as it meets with in the Comet, but also of carrying them off, before they are confumed, to that vaſt Diſtance to which the Tail ſometimes extends.

Where the inflammable Particles are quite con- ſumed, the Tail of the Comet muſt end; and the electric Matter will afterwards be inviſibly diſperſed thro' the planetary Regions, where it may be gathered up by the Planets in their Courſes round the Sun. For ſince we find this kind of Matter placed in all Bodies by the Wiſdom of Providence, we muſt conclude it is neceſſary for carrying on the ſeveral Operations of Nature; and we know it is very apt to eſcape from Bodies by its great Subtilty and repelling Force. We ſee it riſes from the Earth into the Atmoſphere, and is probably going off from thence when it appears in the *Aurora Borealis*. In like Manner it may fly off from the other Planets, and be continually expanding itſelf from the Center of our Syſtem beyond the Orbit of *Saturn*. So that it may be neceſſary it ſhould be brought back again and diſ- perſed among us by the Comets. And it ſeems to me more probable that Comets were intend- ed for this Uſe, than for that of ſupplying the Planets with Moiſture, as Sir *Iſaac Newton* thought. His Opinion was founded on a Suppoſition that all Vegetables have their Growth and Increaſe

R 2   entirely

entirely from Water, and that since they do not turn again into Water but into Earth, there muft be a continual Decay of Moifture, and therefore a frefh Supply of it muft be neceffary from time to time.* But this Suppofition does not feem to have been fufficiently grounded on Experience. For, fince Sir *Ifaac* wrote, Dr. *Woodward*, an ingenious Phyfician, made feveral Experiments on Water and Vegetables growing from it. He fhews that all Water contains an earthy Matter, and concludes: ' It is evident therefore, that Water ' is not the Matter that compofes vegetable Bodies; ' but is the Agent that conveys that Matter ' to them, that introduces, and diftributes ' it to the feveral Parts for their Nourifh- ' ment. Where the proper terreftrial Matter ' is wanting, the Plant is not augmented tho' ' never fo much Water afcends into it.'† This is alfo the Opinion of Dr. *Boerhaave*, and he affirms from his own Experience, that pure elementary Water cannot, by repeated Diftillations,

or

---

* Nam Vegetabilia omnia ex Liquoribus *omnino* crefcunt, dein magna ex parte in Terram aridam per Putrefactionem abeunt, & Limus ex Liquoribus putrefactis perpetuo decidit. Hinc moles Terræ aridæ indies augetur, & Liquores, nifi aliunde augmentum fumerent, perpetuo decrefcere deberent, ac tandem deficere. *Principia,* Pag. 515. Edit. 2da.

† *Philof. Tranfactions.* No. 253.

or otherwise, be converted into Earth.‡ So that there seems to be no Necessity for supposing a gradual Decay of Moisture in any of the Planets. Besides, if the Comets were intended to supply the Planets with Moisture, none of them could serve for this Purpose more than once, but must afterwards become useless, tho' they return regularly in their Orbits, which is not agreeable to the Oeconomy of Nature. For when the Heat of the Sun had driven all the Moisture it could from a Comet in its *Perihelion*, where should it afterwards get a fresh Supply? We can scarce suppose the Planets to lose any Moisture by Evaporation, as no Vapours can rise above their Atmospheres. Or even if any very thin Vapours, Steams or Effluvia of a moist Nature should arise from them, they could not have Heat and Elasticity enough to expand themselves very far. But the electric Matter, from its vast subtilty and velocity, seems capable of making great Excursions from the planetary System, and therefore the several Comets in their long excursions from the Sun, in all Directions, may overtake this Matter; and attracting it to themselves may come back replete with it, and being again heated by the Sun may disperse it among the Planets, and so keep up a Circulation of this Matter which we have reason to think it necessary in our System.

Sir

---

‡ *Elements of Chymistry*, Part 2d.

Sir *Isaac*, after giving his Opinion that the aqueous Particles thrown off from Comets are taken up by the Planets as a supply of Moisture, adds : ' I suspect moreover, That that Spirit which is the ' least, but the most subtile and the best Part of ' our Air, and is necessary for supporting the Life ' of all Things, comes chiefly from the Comets.'† which shews that he thought the Tails of Comets consisted of something more than watery Clouds and Vapours. What he meant by these Words I cannot say with Certainty, but I think they are extremely applicable to that kind of Matter which I have supposed comes to us from the Comets ; and with which our Air generally abounds.

I shall now recapitulate, in a few Words, the Substance of what has been said. As the Tail of a Comet, tho' exceedingly rare, yet meets with no Resistance in its rapid Motion round the Sun, (except so slight a one as can only cause a very small Condensation on that Side of it which moves foremost, and thereby may make it a little brighter than the other Side) it cannot possibly move in a *Medium* denser and heavier than itself, and therefore

† Porro suspicor Spiritum illum qui Aeris nostri pars minima est, sed subtilissima & optima, & ad rerum omnium vitam requiritur ex Cometis præcipue venire. *Principia*, Pag. 515.

fore cannot be raifed up from the Sun by the fuperior Gravity of fuch a *Medium*. And fince the Tail
is not capable of reflecting or refracting the Light
of the Stars, it cannot fhine by reflecting the Sun's
Light; and confequently does not confift of Clouds
or aqueous Vapours, but is itfelf a fhining Subftance. And from what Aftronomers fay of the
Splendor of Comets' Tails, I am perfuaded they
do not fhine with fuch a dull Light, as would be
reflected to us by Clouds or Vapours at fo great a
Diftance, but with a brifker, tho' a glimmering
Light, fuch as would arife from a very thin volatile burning Matter. And here I muft not omit
an Obfervation of Dr. *Halley*'s, which feems very
much to my Purpofe. In his Defcription of the
remarkable *Aurora Borealis* feen in *England* in the
Year 1716, (which I mentioned before) fpeaking
of the great Streams of Light, he fays : *They fo*
much refembled the long Tails of Comets, that at firft
Sight they might well be taken for fuch. And afterwards, *This Light feems to have a great Affinity to*
that which the Effluvia of electric Bodies emit in the
Dark.§ From whence we find that this accurate
Obferver perceived a Refemblance between thofe
Subftances that I have been comparing together.
Now I have fhewn that they agree remarkably, not
only in their Appearance, but alfo in fuch Properties as we can obferve in each of them, and therefore

fore I have fuppofed them to be Subftances of the fame Nature, I have alfo endeavoured to fhew that the electric Matter, from its known Properties, is capable of exhibiting to us all the Phænomena of Comets' Tails, and that we may from thence affign the Ufe of Comets with more Probability than has hitherto been done. By this Account, if it fhould happen to be a true one, we fhall avoid all thofe Objections that have been made to the *Newtonian* Doctrine of a *Vacuum* in the celeftial Spaces, from the Afcent and Bending of Comets' Tails. For the electric Matter is far too rare and fubtile to give any Refiftance to the Motion of large and denfe Bodies, as we find it paffes thro' them with as much Eafe as thro' a Vacuum. And thefe Obfervations, by tending to fhew the Univerfality of this kind of Matter, may encourage us to further Enquiries into its Nature and Properties; from a Knowledge of which I fufpect our future Improvements in Natural Philofophy will chiefly arife; efpecially in that Part of it which relates to Fire and Heat, the Nature of which is at prefent but little known.

F I N I S.